DYLAN

DYLAN

by

SIDNEY MICHAELS

Based on

Dylan Thomas in America

by John Malcolm Brinnin

and

Leftover Life to Kill

by Caitlin Thomas

Random House   *New York*

Preface

In the dark of the theatre we remember ourselves. And we know we are not average men and that Madison Avenue shall not sell us that we are. In the inner space of the theatre, our blood turns red. Our nerves signal us again, as via Telstar, directly across the ocean of the orchestra pit, straight to the pit of our stomachs with the pitiless speed of feeling which, if not faster, is more revealing than light.

In the bell and siren of the theatre, the dormant half of the brain wakes up. Speaks up, saying, "Who the hell can identify with ordinary men?" For none of us is ordinary to ourselves. And it is to ourselves that we awaken, in the morning of the theatre. Nobody is Joe Doakes, but everybody is Hamlet—prince, insane, with murders to commit, with trap-door graves of Ophelia-loves to leap into, with wit and poetry on the tongue's apt tip. And everybody is Falstaff, gross drunk, thief, liar, scoundrel, lead-weight clown, tipable but up-popable, whose windbag blarney has a quotable beauty. All men want to turn a flower girl into a princess. And all women, once having been turned, want to turn about and tell the teacher off. And both may relish having the mind of Shaw to do it with.

In the free country of the theatre, our private selves are as differing pearls that yet hang integrated on a one strand, the force that through us runs and tethers us up together, be it called Heart or Soul or God or Being, but that enables us to seat ourselves all facing one way and pray for miracles; and if the miracle is laughter, up goes the general roar, and if the miracle is tears, out come a thousand handkerchiefs and dab two thousand eyes, and if the miracle is terror, we all have our hearts in our throats at once, and we share the fear, and the courage to face the fear, just as we do when our President takes a-life-or-death stand in our name and we spill over with pride and are shoveled full of the fuel of love, and we are never more solidly alive or crisply human. For weeks after the fire-ice event, we stride in boots, and our lives have meaning; we are newborn and the air seems cleaner, for we have identified with an action which is just and courageous, and beautiful to us for those reasons. The theatre is not one speck a thing less than that.

True, if as we walked about in the usual slim of day, we were to act like beanstalk giants, we'd be abruptly hoosegowed by the society whose Jacklike modesty we'd shaken. But that does *not* mean that if there is *no* place where we can go and remember ourselves, we won't equally endanger that society by corroding it from within, sickening the whole apple because the core has gone brown and rots. We have as good a need, genuine as a gene, to partake of that sweet resurrecting occasion that nourishes us, in the survival kit of the theatre, as good a need as a bum has for his nightcap, a child for making shadows on the wall, or men and women for the love and respect of one another.

In the weightless crater of the theatre: that is where Hamlet's palace is, and Lear's asylum moor, and the town square of Thebes. There grows the cherry orchard. And there stands the butternut tree. And over it flies a wild duck. And a sea gull. And a bluebird. That's where Desire lies to which the streetcar ran. And Willy's Brooklyn with its skeleton house and encroaching apartments. And that's where the bus stop is and the girl who lives upstairs of the summer bachelor. And the French planter and the Navy nurse are raising their Polynesian children there.

And that is where we live. In the reality of the theatre. Not in the fiction of society. But where we can identify. Where we are extraordinary. Where we speak like angels, feel like saints and act like heroes. Where life is as romantic and true as the telescopes tell us. Where we remember ourselves. In the passionate, compassionate tall, large, deep, bright, dark of the theatre.

So may this one play called *Dylan,* prove to be, I most fervently pray and hope, of these foretold pretensions of its author, even somewhat a reflection, and fulfillment. And to reader, listener, looker-on, may it convey my vigorous and unassassinatable respect for all the uncommon things we have in common.

DYLAN *was first presented by George W. George and Frank Granat at the Plymouth Theatre, New York City, on January 18, 1964, with the following cast:*

(In order of appearance)

CAITLIN	Kate Reid
DYLAN	Alec Guinness
REPORTERS	Louisa Cabot
	Janet Sarno
	Susan Wills
	Carol Gustafson
	Grant Code
	Paul Larson
	Jonathan Moore
BRINNIN	James Ray
ANGUS	Martin Garner
CLUBWOMAN	Susan Willis
MEG	Barbara Berjer
ANNABELLE	Jenny O'Hara
MATTOCK	Gordon B. Clarke
BARTENDER	Paul Larson
STAGE MANAGER	Jonathan Moore
BYSTANDER	Ernest Graves
KATHERINE ANNE PORTER	Carol Gustafson
MISS WONDERLAND	Louisa Cabot
STAGEHAND	Paul Larson
MINISTER	Grant Code
ELENA	Margaret Braidwood
JAY HENRY	Ernest Graves
DOCTOR	Grant Code

| NANCY | Janet Sarno |
| DECK OFFICER | Jonathan Moore |

Directed by Peter Glenville

Settings by Oliver Smith

Incidental music by Laurence Rosenthal

Costumes by Ruth Morley

Lighting by Jack Brown

The entire action of the play takes place in the early 1950's, in America and Wales.

Act One

ACT I

The sound of the ocean. A cork-hung fish net acts as a scrim curtain through which we see a beach on the west coast of Wales. Under a boathouse set up on spiles a curly-haired, button-nosed, unneat but oddly compelling man in a turtle-neck sweater sits on a flight of steps staring up at all the winter stars. A cigarette dangles from his lips, curling smoke. The fish net lifts into a scalloped drapery framing the setting. Down the flight of steps comes a blond woman in her mid and attractive thirties, in a great-coat, and sits two steps above the man.

The man is DYLAN THOMAS. The woman is his wife, CAITLIN. She has an Irish accent. He speaks a "cut-glass British."

CAITLIN So here you are, you scum.

DYLAN Don't try to make up. It's too late.

CAITLIN Do you know *how* late, Dylan?

DYLAN So late, it's early. All the Welsh and welching stars about to slide shut like the top of a spice tin. That's a sick star, Cat—*that* one—tell you how you can tell—it's shining brighter than every other star—it's about to explode!

CAITLIN It's cold down here on the beach.

DYLAN As a witch's tit.

CAITLIN You be sure to take out insurance before you get on the plane.

DYLAN   I *have* insurance. My poems will bring in an income for years.

CAITLIN   Two shillings, rain or shine.

DYLAN   Nobody asked you to marry a penniless poet.

CAITLIN   Somebody must have. It isn't the kind of thing I could have dreamt up all by myself.

DYLAN   What have you got on under that cheap imitation dog's fur?

CAITLIN   My bikini.

DYLAN   In February? Go up and change. You're out of season.

CAITLIN   I won't!

DYLAN   You will!

CAITLIN   I'll do as I bloody please. The only little pleasure I get any more is to put this on and parade around the boathouse imagining myself to be married to a man who could afford to take me to a warm climate.

DYLAN   Like to hell.

CAITLIN   Or Majorca!

DYLAN   You're very grand.

CAITLIN   I come by it very naturally.

DYLAN   Naturally. Your father was a friend of Augustus John! Here we go again!

CAITLIN Who's had precious few intimates, and he's a *very* famous man. Why, the whole *world* knows who Augustus John is. And his remarkable portraits fetched a very fancy price and still do to this day.

DYLAN I can't help it if an ignorant civilization sets more store by a painted patch of pocky canvas than it does by a singing heart. I'll come off better 'n he will in a thousand years.

CAITLIN It takes too long.

DYLAN Look at the Bible.

CAITLIN Look at the pyramids.

DYLAN You look at the pyramids; I'll look at the Bible.

CAITLIN Nobody in Wales, nobody in your home town here even knows who you are.

DYLAN How do you ask for me?

CAITLIN I go about saying, "Who here knows my husband, Dylan Thomas, the poet?"

DYLAN Well, no wonder. I'm not known as the poet. In my home town I'm known as the drunk. It's my principal ambition. "What do you want to be when you grow up, young Dylan?" my father'd say to me. And I'd say to my father, "Daddy, I want to be the drunkest man in the world!"

CAITLIN It's the thing you do best. Where were you all night? And your last night home, you scum.

DYLAN   You knew where I was. You might have joined me. I was at Brown's Hotel. Having a quiet brew or two in Ivy Williams' pub. Enjoying your absence and the company of some of my earthy friends. Real people. People who work, who dig ditches. Fishermen. Whores. The kind of people Christ used to pal about with.

CAITLIN   Oh, Christ!

DYLAN   That's it. Shout your profanity to the bloody town!

CAITLIN   I suppose you entertained the lot of 'em describing the battle royal we had in the afternoon.

DYLAN   Not at all. Why should it've come up? (*Pause*) Though I must say they thought it middling strange that just before her dear husband's embarking on a distant journey to America, a wife wants no part of his last legal lust-legitimate offer to pin her down, flat and happy, on her flip-flop vernacular.

CAITLIN   Not in the afternoon.

DYLAN   And why not?

CAITLIN   Because it's not proper.

DYLAN   We always used to do it in the afternoon.

CAITLIN   A lady does it at night.

DYLAN   Or blindfolded.

CAITLIN   So you spent twelve hours discussing our private sex life with whores and fishermen, did you?

6

DYLAN I wasn't discussing *our* private sex life. I was using the third person all the way. I was referring to it along the lines of would *a* woman wed to *a* man for too goddam many years and after three children . . .

CAITLIN (*Interrupting*) Four, counting you.

DYLAN Well, I never once let on it was my own story. Isn't the tip of your nose frostbit? The tip of something of mine is. Let's go to bed.

CAITLIN I'd rather die first. You scum!

DYLAN If you say you scum once more, I'll kick you right in the teeth. I know the real reason you're up in arms. Or not up in *my* arms. Not up and down in my seesaw arms.

CAITLIN Oh, stop singing!

DYLAN It's my going away tomorrow. Today, I should say to be accurate.

CAITLIN Dylan, if you go to America tomorrow, I'll never go to bed with you again.

DYLAN Don't make threats you can't possibly keep, Cat. You know how not to be denied I am.

CAITLIN Not in the morning, not in the afternoon, not at night—

DYLAN (*Quotes her*) "Because all the college girls in America are whores!"

CAITLIN   You'll get syphilis right on the campus!

DYLAN   Driven to it from sexual neglect.

CAITLIN   They wear bobby sox and no panties.

DYLAN   Where did you hear that?

CAITLIN   Read Faulkner, read Thomas Wolfe!

DYLAN   You read too bloody much. So all the money we're going to make is meaningless suddenly. Six months' solid lecture-tour bookings: so much—Alka-Seltzer.

CAITLIN   You won't come back with a penny.

DYLAN   I *will* come back with a penny. I'll be being wined and dined. I'm going to be patronized.

CAITLIN   You'll drink too much there.

DYLAN   I can't. I've got to get up on a lecture platform practically every night and read my poems. I can't do that stinking, can I? (*She tosses him a look*) Well, if I do, they'll spot it, and I'll be packed home in a week. We have nothing to lose and the world to gain. We've won the American sweepstakes!

CAITLIN   You only want to get away from home. You're a selfish brute. You don't give an f'ing damn about me. You go off Scot-free, abandoning me! Trapped in this ugly, dull, ice-cold, bourgeois, buggy little seaside cesspool, next door to your father and mother who cringe if I whistle.

DYLAN It isn't your whistling makes them cringe; it's your entertaining seven truck drivers while I was in London last with nothing between their popped eyes and your bare white body but a black lace slip with sequins on it!

CAITLIN I have to have *some* fun! Just like you when you trot off and leave me here, glued night and day to three Dylan-aping, time-sucking brats. And where's me? Where's my personal self in all this? I mean, whatever became of Miss Caitlin McNamara of Dublin's fair city? Do you know how long it's been since I danced?

DYLAN Foxtrot?

CAITLIN Don't be funny. Since I set foot on a public platform and just danced for people. To applause. You don't realize it, goddam it, Dylan—

DYLAN I'm aware of it.

CAITLIN But I was a rather extraordinary modern dancer and I held great promise. I was a highly paid artist's model, too. I sat for Augustus John. I even had a certain talent for caricature and might have made my way in the very lucrative cartooning field. And I wrote a little myself, if you still recall. Oh, God, but I sound so pitiful hauling out my notices like a has-been vaudevillian, but I was very good at *all* the arts and I didn't go on with *any* of it and the years just shot by and here I am, to look forward to six months without my husband, without money, without help.

DYLAN You've *got* help.

CAITLIN   The help we've got is no help at all. I have to help *her!*

DYLAN   Then fire her, damn it.

CAITLIN   I can't fire her, Dylan. We owe her six months' back wages.

DYLAN   Well, if you wouldn't push her down the stairs like you did twice last week, she'd be more helpful.

CAITLIN   They love being pushed downstairs.

DYLAN   Who's "they"?

CAITLIN   The *help.*

DYLAN   Goddam it—that's snotty as hell!

CAITLIN   I don't care. I don't give a damn—about anything. I'm all alone and I'm trapped. I should have been a man. (*The anger ebbs suddenly, a pause and then softly*) How much time is there left us?

DYLAN   I have to catch the seven o'clock train to London in time for my flight.

CAITLIN (*A realization*)   My rival. My rival. The whole nation of America.

DYLAN   I've no time to think about romantic twaddle now. All I can think about now is money. Like every other poet since time began. I tell you, I must be growing up or something. And I don't like it. I'm scared. I'm

scared to the bone. I used to look like some f'ng angel
or something. In my cherubim-twenties, when your
great Augustus John pled with me to pose for him,
around the day you were so wild to have met me, the
very year Dame Edith Sitwell up'd and said I was the
only lyric poet of the twentieth century and, my God, I
really didn't think I was *that* good, but I suppose she
knew what she was talking about. Well, it all came
easier. Came easier and went easier. The beer went
down easier, it was easier breathing. I've got uglier
now. I've put on weight like a man who's middle-aged.
My hair's darker. I'm dirtier and smaller. The callus
on my finger from the pencil's big as an egg. Stained.
Cigarettes. From hack work—for money—for travelogues
—for writing "as we sail off into the sunset and leave the
beautiful Isle of Birdspit." (*Pause*) I haven't written a
new poem in a terribly long time. Take the last BBC
broadcast I did; d'you know, Cat, I was suddenly aware
there I was reading the best of me and it was all fifteen-
year-old stuff. If I don't write a new poem soon, I'll die—
of boredom. Of I don't know. Of rage.

CAITLIN (*Urgently*) I don't care if we starve, then. Don't
go there. Don't go to America. You should be sitting up
there in the shack, Dylan, working on new poems. That's
what you do, Dylan. But they'll turn you into a per-
former. They'll make you into a clown for interviews
and buy your so available soul with paper money! I
mean, Ford Motors and duPont and the United States
Marine Corps. All those monopolies!

DYLAN I love monopoly. It's my favorite game of chance.

I have to grow up and get to play it on the big boy's board. I have to earn a living someday, don't I? What are Llewellyn and Aeron and Colm to think of their dandy father if he can't send them three to college like a father's supposed to do? I'm their only father. I'm somebody's provident daddy, for Christ's sake. I can't go on playing bully-boy poet when the hairs in my ears and nostrils have begun to gray. And what else am I fitted for? In Wales. In England. To be poor and famous as a *Wunderkind*? Some kind of a Celtic nut? Well, it's high time I acted my chronological age. I'm a man thirty-eight years old. I'd better become a man of letters by forty or go to work as a bartender, something I know about. (*Pause*) John Malcolm Brinnin writes that I'm a legend in America. He says I'm an influence. That I'm taught there in classrooms. And they're all rich as Croesus there. Why, Texas sophomores who memorized me fifteen years ago have shot their fathers in saloons by now and taken over the oil wells. He writes they're perishing to see me in the flesh—well, they're going to pay to see me in the flesh. And by the pound. A teaching position at a university. A sinecure. Miami Beach University, for instance. Where you could get out in the sun in that vulgar G-string. Get those three brats out in the sun and bake the perennial flu out of them. Don't stop me. Don't stop me, Cat. You wait and see. You're going to be proud of me. We're going to be rich. Adults. With respect. And live sensibly. Cut down on the liquor a lot, too. I can't write if I drink. Well? Well, optimism just pinched your ass. Why don't you smile?

(CAITLIN *wrestles herself into a begrudging but finally glowing smile. And then wistfully*)

CAITLIN Oh, Dylan, it would be worth losing you even for six months, if we could really lift our heads and see daylight at last.

DYLAN Now you're talking, Cat. America, why, America is our salvation.

CAITLIN Do you really think it can work?

DYLAN I do. I do. We'll bank it this time, so help me, God.

CAITLIN (*Smiles*) Oh, Mr. Thomas. Won't you, won't you say the poem you wrote for me the week we married?

DYLAN What a fantasy! I only finished it that week. I began it nearly a year before that. I didn't write anything the week we married and damn little since.

CAITLIN Well, then, forget it!

DYLAN All right, I'll do it. Light us two cigarettes. (*She does*) I can use the practice for my American audiences so it won't be a total loss.

CAITLIN You know, for a sensitive man, you're a hateful, rotten, insensitive son-of-a-bitch.

DYLAN You ever wear that f'ing bikini out of the house again, I'll make you black and blue for a month!

CAITLIN You talk about growing up in one breath and you still don't know how to blow your nose. You scum!

DYLAN Shut up!
(*He slaps her*)

CAITLIN   Shut up yourself!

> (*She wallops him back. There is a long pause. They stare at each other. The stars have gone by now. The sun is up and glowing. Seagulls are crying overhead*)

DYLAN   Let me see. It begins:

"Now, as I was young and easy under the apple boughs
About the lilting house and happy as the grass was green,
    The night above the dingle starry,
        Time let me hail and climb
    Golden in the heydays of his eyes,
And honored among wagons I was prince of the apple
        towns
And once below a time I lordly had the trees and leaves
        Trail with daisies and barley
    Down the rivers of the windfall light.

"And as I was green and carefree, famous among the
        barns
About the happy yard and singing as the farm was home,
    In the sun that is young once only,
        Time let me play and be
    Golden in the mercy of his means,
And green and golden I was huntsman and herdsman,
        the calves
Sang to my horn, the foxes on the hills barked clear and
        cold,
        And the sabbath rang slowly
    In the pebbles of the holy streams."

CAITLIN   (*She has turned and faces him*) That is so beautiful. That's so beautiful, Dylan.

DYLAN

DYLAN Oh, Cat, if you really love the talent, you've got to love the opportunity that's about to come true for it.

CAITLIN I'm so afraid they'll change you, Dylan.

DYLAN Never! My personality's tattoo'd. It won't come off.

CAITLIN They'll try, Dylan. I love you the way you are— stubborn and funny and ratty old Dylan down to your boots. (*Pause*) Do I have to ask to be held?

DYLAN Come here. Come here. (*Takes her in his arms*) Get in there where the fat's cooking that'll keep you warm.

CAITLIN What a bright day it's going to be.

DYLAN It is.

CAITLIN You can see miles out into the estuary already.

DYLAN Can you?

CAITLIN Don't forget to go to a dentist the second you land in New York. You'll be a toothless lion before you're forty.

DYLAN Will you love me as a toothless lion?

CAITLIN I've no pride in you, Dylan—just emotional attachment. I don't think there's any end to it.

DYLAN Oh, Caitlin! Cat! You're the only girl for me. The only girl I'll ever love till the day I explode and go out like a light.

CAITLIN   Oh, Dylan, Dylan—hurry up!

(He takes her in his arms and kisses her. Then, he walks her up to home and bed and good-bye; the lights go down and the tumult of DYLAN's journey to America begins. In the dark, the airplane roars that carries him there. Lights.

The scene is Idlewild Airport in New York. Just outside customs, on the steel-ribbed ramp leading to the main terminal. DYLAN and REPORTERS are in a pad-and-pencil cluster)

DYLAN   *(Machine-gun delivery)*   Idlewild is a fine definition of a poet's goals—to be wild and to be idle.

REPORTER   *(How to pronounce it?)*   Dullen or Dylan?

DYLAN   Dylan. As in penicillin. I used to be a reporter myself. Sent out, God love me, to cover sporting events about which I knew nothing except to sit at the ringside and yell, "Kick him again!" You might say poets are reporters of sporting events of the human heart, of what took place the other night in the spotlit head of the beholder, at the arterial ringside, having a bloody good time.

REPORTER   "Arterial?"

DYLAN   ". . . ringside, having a bloody good time."

REPORTER   How was your flight?

DYLAN   Excellent. I very nearly suffocated, it was so bloody hot.

REPORTER Were your fellow passengers aware presence?

DYLAN My fellow passengers were a forbidding ᴵᵒᵗ gnomes, international spies and Presbyterians.

REPORTER How do you like America?

DYLAN I don't believe it for a minute. You're all living in a dream. I wouldn't wake you up for the world.

WOMAN REPORTER Do you believe in God?

DYLAN I'd be a damn fool if I didn't.

REPORTER How about *Freud*?

DYLAN How *about* Freud! Whatever is hidden should be made naked—brought to light—to clarity.

REPORTER Speaking of clarity. Some of us, Dylan, have had trouble understanding your poems.

DYLAN Then you should read Robert Frost.

WOMAN REPORTER I understand you're going to be here six months. How does your wife feel about that?

DYLAN Dear Caitlin. Quaint, quiet woman; never ventures an opinion.

REPORTER Did you get to see the New York skyline from the plane?

DYLAN I did. I did. Of course, it's all a mistake, you understand, but it's too late for us to do anything about it.

Let's all go have a stiff drink on the boily boy. Somebody bring cash. Somebody find a pub. Somebody go get my luggage. It's two string-tied, tongue-tied bags of thin hide, hideous to see. Malcolm Brinnin is due to pick me up. The late John Malcolm Brinnin. Not dead but tardy. He'll reimburse you all. It's out of my pocket. He's the Irish director of the Jewish Poetry Center and he's just begun to import Welsh poets, which is a hobby he may live to regret!

> (*A tall, fair-haired young man*—JOHN MALCOLM BRINNIN—*walks hastily on*)

REPORTER What decided you to come to America, Dylan?

DYLAN To continue my lifelong search for naked women in wet mackintoshes. Who has a cigar?

BRINNIN (*Extending a large cigar*) I do. I'm John Malcolm Brinnin.

DYLAN Thank God, Brinnin, you're just in time. I'm totally inarticulate when it comes to interviews.
> (*They start to walk away*)

REPORTERS At the birdie, Mr. T.
Life of the party!
Have a heart.
That's it!
Freeze!
> (DYLAN *and* BRINNIN *exit*)
We'll get him in the bar!
Pie-eyed!
Get him fried.

Better yet.

Let's go!

Break out the gin.

Look out, New York. Our annual wild Welsh poet just breezed in.

C'mon, I'll buy you a drink.

>(As they walk off the lights go down.
>
>The time is three days later. It is morning in a Manhattan hotel room. BRINNIN and ANGUS MARIUS, an owlish, dwarfish American publisher, confer in violent whispers. From time to time, with exasperated gestures, they indicate their subject matter, DYLAN, crumped out in a lump of sleep under a mound of covers on the bed. Coffee and Danish are on a tray. ANGUS butters a Danish with whiplike fury)

ANGUS   All I know is—as one of the first people to publish Dylan Thomas in this country, I have certain inalienable rights in his social calendar, and ever since he arrived, there's been no attempt, none, to bring him together with me.

BRINNIN   He was lost, Angus. I took him to see the top of the RCA Building.

ANGUS   Where you promptly proceeded to lose him.

BRINNIN   Didn't you ever lose somebody?

ANGUS   Not for three days.

BRINNIN   I didn't lose him on purpose.

19

ANGUS   But did you call me? Did you say, "Angus, I've
lost Dylan Thomas"? Did you call the civic authorities
and say, "I am responsible here for a Welsh poet—he's
missing for three days. I am guilty of having taken him
to see the top of the RCA Building"?

BRINNIN   He asked to see it!

ANGUS   What does he know? He's in a strange country.
He needs guidance. This is a major event in world litera-
ture. This is the coming to America of Dylan Thomas.
It will be discussed and gone over for a hundred critical
years—and look whose wishy-washy hands it's in. John
Malcolm Brinnin, the Eisenhower of modern poetry.

BRINNIN   In a minute I'm going to throw the Peter Lorre
of modern poetry out that window, which will be of no
interest whatsoever for a hundred critical years.

ANGUS   I had two important cocktail parties lined up for
him, at which he didn't show.

BRINNIN   You didn't check them with me.

ANGUS   Well, I've got one lined up Tuesday night after
his first reading at the Y.

BRINNIN   Check it with me.

ANGUS   I'm doing that right now. Is that all right with
you, Mr. Brinnin?

BRINNIN   Quite all right, Mr. Marius.

ANGUS   You know, I don't mind checking with you if you're going to be in charge like a person who's in charge, but if you're going to lose the poet you imported out of the RCA building, I don't see why I have to check anything with you.

BRINNIN   I'm not his mother, Angus.

ANGUS   Prove it! You assumed the position of being responsible for him—you can't suddenly throw him out to his own devices. Are you his man here, or aren't you?
    (*Pause*)

BRINNIN   I guess I am. In a sense.

ANGUS   Well, you better be. He's telling everybody he meets you are. I introduced him to Myra Coots and the first thing he said to Myra was—

BRINNIN   When? You just told me you hadn't had a chance to see him.

ANGUS   Well, I ran into him in the Village two days ago.

BRINNIN   So that's where he's been. With you and your endless string of sluts!

ANGUS   That's a forest fire; you want it to behave like your cigarette lighter!

BRINNIN   Stop putting me in the position of the madman's maiden aunt.

ANGUS   Then stop putting me in the position of the town pimp. The girls I introduced Dylan to were all college graduates.

BRINNIN Don't you realize, Angus, if he doesn't turn in a solid decent performance at the Y Tuesday, the whole tour's over? Every university I've set up for him'll have a spy there. If Dylan's looped or pooped or dull or inaudible, the cancellations'll pour in in the morning. You don't seem to grasp what's going on here, Angus. He's broke. He needs money. And I tell you—Dylan's reputation for irresponsible behavior is a very living legend. So I found myself elected.

ANGUS Self-elected is right. I could have arranged a piddling tour of some dozen campuses as easily as you. I could have gotten Sol Hurok to book him. The whole affair is amateur night.

BRINNIN All right, and maybe this lump on the bed, this forest fire, will come to loathe me for it. I may possibly end up loathing myself. But I intend to try my damnedest to make him a big success and a little money in America. Don't ask me why I'm doing it. It just seems like somebody should. I only ask that you leave him alone till after his first reading. Just so my piddling tour can at least have a chance to piddle. Above and beyond that, I'm not my brother's keeper.

ANGUS You'll live to eat those words. Let me give you one last piece of advice.

BRINNIN Good God!

ANGUS When you've got a tiger by the tail, don't try to teach it table manners.

BRINNIN That forest fire, that tiger, that hangover there in the bed is a frightened child of thirty-eight.

ANGUS (*In flourishing disagreement*) The oldest man alive!

BRINNIN How about lovable bastard? Would you agree with that?

ANGUS Now, you're talking. The Good Joe of Geniuses.

DYLAN (*Sits up—fully dressed*) That's me, by God! A lovable bastard! And the sweetest fella you'll ever want to meet!
    (ANGUS *and* BRINNIN, *embarrassed, glance at each other*)

ANGUS How much of our conversation, Dylan, did you lie there listening to?

DYLAN Does a forest fire have ears? Does a tiger understand English?

BRINNIN You're due at one o'clock at a luncheon.

DYLAN (*Jumps out of bed*) Absolutely. I'm already dressed. But I don't want to miss breakfast. Call room service. I'll have a double bourbon with a raw egg in it.
    (*The lights go down, then come up as* DYLAN *walks forward to a fat, blue-haired* CLUBWOMAN *standing at a microphone. She wears an incredible hat, mostly flowers*)

CLUBWOMAN This has been a thrilling experience, a privilege to meet you, for all of us here this afternoon.

DYLAN   Not at all, madam.

CLUBWOMAN   Your impressions of New York are so—lusty and significant.

DYLAN   The rather customary awe of any country boy come to the big city.

CLUBWOMAN   Well, we're all coming Tuesday to the reading with our tickets clutched in our hot little hands.

DYLAN   Goody.

CLUBWOMAN   Now, you've told us what you think of America and poetry and God. What do you think of the Greater New York Chapter of the American National Poetry Appreciation Center?

DYLAN   Madam, the creamed chicken was more than swell, the punch has left me wordless, and *you* are not to be believed but I believe you, believe you me.

> (*The lights go down, then come up on a corner of the White Horse Tavern. There is a rustic table, hanging iron chandeliers, a statue of a white horse on the mantelpiece—a generally gewgawed smoked-over aura.* ANGUS *comes on with two pretty girls,* MEG STUART *and* ANNABELLE GRAHAM-PIKE. MEG *is older and commanding and well endowed.* ANNA-BELLE *will grow up to be fat but is now collegiate and cute as a button with the vocabulary of a drunken sailor*)

ANGUS   Girls, this is the White Horse Tavern. The Horse, Dylan calls it. Let me ask the old man here if he's been and gone.

(*He walks over to the bar. The two girls,* MEG *and* ANNABELLE, *sit down at a table. A* WAITER *comes over*)

MEG (*To the* WAITER) I'll have a dry vodka martini with a twist. Mr. Marius'll have Scotch on the rocks. She'll have—a pink lady.

ANNABELLE (*Astonished*) That's my drink!

MEG When I went to Smith, there was a girl just like you and it was *her* drink. It's a very sweet sweet sweet drink. I hear.

ANNABELLE Yes, it is.

ANGUS (*Returns*) No, he hasn't pulled in yet.

MEG Are you so sure he'll want liquor before tonight's performance?

ANGUS The Las Vegas odds, my dear Meg—

MEG I see. Then, we're in for a disaster. I may not go.
(*The* WAITER *returns with the drinks and sets them on the table*)

ANGUS It won't be dull. That's a promise. That's Dylan's sacred word to the world. That's the only word he keeps. It won't be dull. (*Reacting to* ANNABELLE'S *choice of drink*) Annabelle, what *is that?*
(*The* WAITER *exits*)

ANNABELLE The goddam thing is called a pink lady.

ANGUS It's quite sweet, isn't it?

ANNABELLE It's very sweet, Angus. Just like me.

ANGUS Listen, I think you're sweet. You know how sweet *I* think you are.

ANNABELLE Oh, Angus. You're too much.

MEG Is your father writing a new novel, Annabelle?

ANNABELLE The same novel. It just keeps coming out under different titles.

MEG What does he think of Dylan's poetry?

ANNABELLE Words, words, words, he says. He thinks Dylan's a bum. But that's what he said about every one of my mothers. Won't he be surprised when he finds out I've become Dylan's mistress.

MEG Oh? When did that happen?

ANNABELLE As soon as I meet him.

MEG How will your father find out, dear?

ANNABELLE I'm going to shout it from the housetops. I'm a very free, compulsive person. I have no sense of shame. I'm amoral.

MEG. Maybe Mr. Thomas won't want you.

ANNABELLE Oh, yes, he will. I hear he's not at all fussy.

MEG Angus?

ANGUS Don't glare at me. I simply promised Annabelle she could meet him. No more than I promised you, Meg.

I'm really going to stop introducing people to people. The minute they meet they go off and leave me anyway.

ANNABELLE (*To* MEG) Don't *you* want to sleep with Dylan Thomas?

MEG No.

ANNABELLE You *don't?*

MEG With a married drunk—why should I?

ANNABELLE But he's a great poet. Angus says he is. I can't wait to see him in action tonight. They say the sound of his voice is like an organ. Holy, holy, holy. Well, all I can say is I'm available as hell—for Dylan! (*To the* BARTENDER) Hi! (*To the* DRUNK *in the corner*) Hi there!

MEG Maybe he'll get a divorce and marry you.

ANNABELLE Who're you kidding? I'm going to be the mistress of ten great poets and then I'm going to marry a manufacturer and see what's cooking in Rye, New York. Go ahead 'n' laugh. The reason, I tell you, I'll make out with geniuses is because they all drink—they wanta die young—somebody told 'em that's the *Good Housekeeping* seal of approval. And I can outlast any camp follower alive on the round of bars every night. I'm famous for my hollow leg.

MEG *Are* you?

ANNABELLE I'm a bottomless pit!

ANGUS With a pitiless bottom!

ANNABELLE (*Seeing* DYLAN *off stage*) There he is. Just like his photographs!

ANGUS Mattock's with him. A very fine poet. Robert Mattock.

ANNABELLE (*To* MEG) One for us each.

MEG I've retired from the ring. *You* fight.
(DYLAN *enters with* MATTOCK, *who is balancing his teddy-bear weight on a pair of crutches. Both are foggy bright with a day of drinking behind them*)

DYLAN Mattock broke his leg. I'm drunk.
(DYLAN *flops down in a chair*)

ANGUS You don't seem drunk.

DYLAN I am. I'm a button hanging on a frayed thread.

MATTOCK (*Stowing his crutches*) Angus, is it true you married your sister?

ANGUS I had a brother. I never had a sister.

MATTOCK Worse.

ANGUS Gentlemen, Meg Stuart and Annabelle Graham-Pike.

MATTOCK (*To* ANNABELLE) Mainstay of the American Book Club?

ANNABELLE His only child.

ANGUS   Meg's my assistant editor over at Peter Piper Press.

DYLAN (*Off in a private world*)   How do I do. How do I do.

MATTOCK   Usually when you meet a brace of girls, one's nifty and the other's a dog. I have to assume you two never met before tonight to account for the good things coming in bunches.

ANNABELLE   That's right. How astute!

DYLAN (*Comes to life, pounds the table*)   Ass-toot! Beer! Bartender! Beer! Are we in the Horse yet?

MATTOCK   I was just telling Dylan he should send his minor poems to this duchess over in Istanbul. She's paying great money and she has no taste. She buys labels off cans and prints them. (*To the* WAITER) I'll have a small glass of mulled wine. Do you mull your wine around here?

WAITER   We can mull it.

MATTOCK   Then mull me some wine. I'm a man who's broken his leg.

ANGUS   Are you going to have Dylan read at Ohio State? (*To the girls*) Bob teaches at Ohio State.

MATTOCK   Angus, you always sound like you're M.C.ing something. Yes. Dylan's coming to meet the girls in my poetry classes. But at the moment I'm consumed with self-pity. Or is it *Weltschmerz?* I may be crippled for life. I'm in intolerable pain.

ANGUS What's the doctor say happened to you?

MATTOCK He calls it a sprained ankle but what the hell do doctors know about medicine?

DYLAN Bartender! Four double Scotches. I'm running out of time.

MEG You have to read, remember?

DYLAN I don't have to do anything I don't want to do. I can read blind!

ANNABELLE How exceptional!
        (*The* WAITER *brings the drinks*)

DYLAN I'm not exceptional. Ordinary people—I generally hit it off with ordinary people—because I'm one of them and they sense it immediately. I mean, I'm only a poet by accident. (*Drinks*) I don't have any emotions other people don't have. Isn't that right, Angus?

ANGUS Dylan, slow down.

DYLAN I asked you a civil question.

ANGUS You're right.

DYLAN Isn't that right, Mattock?

MATTOCK Hell, no. You're a man with two heads. Any good drunk such as me can spot a man with two heads.

DYLAN (*Drinks*) Where's all my drinks? What the hell—where'd my drinks go? I dropped a drink.

ANGUS You *had* them, Dylan.

DYLAN I want more! *More drinks!*

MATTOCK Let's blow the joint, Dylan. You're due at the Y.M.H.A. in less'n an hour now.

DYLAN No! I like it here in the Horse! I am very fond of everybody here! (*Drinks*) I am very fond of you, Angus. (*To* MATTOCK *and* ANNABELLE) And you. And you. (*To* MEG) Why are you drawn back from me, madam? Do I disgust you? I'm not fond of you. You've got a poker up your ass! Did anybody ever tell you that? You've got a smug hard Salem-bitch look about you. Are you lesbian by chance? Hail to thee, lead weight, bird thou never wert. I'm gonna squeeze your boobs!

ANGUS Dylan, ye gods.

DYLAN (*Pinches her breasts*) Squeak! Squeak! (MEG *just stares at him*) Well, slap my face! I daresay I've got it coming. Well?

MEG (*Slowly*) Don't—do—that—again.

DYLAN No doubt you feel I've grown a trifle too familiar. But I intend to die before I'm forty and I wouldn't want to miss anything. Miss Stuart, your tits are couplets. And now stand up and show us your villanelle!

ANGUS Dylan, have some black coffee.

DYLAN   No.

MATTOCK   You've got to read tonight, Dylan. There's a piece of change riding on it.

DYLAN   I'll be brilliant! I'll be brilliant! (*To* ANNABELLE) Where shall we two meet again?

ANNABELLE   I'll see you at the party later.

DYLAN   Great! Where's the party? You're all invited to a party. 'T's a private party. Everybody's gonna take out his privates. (*He turns to* MEG *and squeezes her again*) Beep! Beep!

ANGUS (*Grabs his hands*)   Dylan, my dear boy, we don't do that.

DYLAN   It isn't being done, you mean? 'Nother drink!

MATTOCK   Save room, Dylan, there'll be lots of booze afterwards at the party.

DYLAN   At the wonderful party in *my* honor. I deserve it. I come along once in a thousand years. I'm unique. I'm a unique eunuch. I'm the only iniquitous, unique eunuch who can play "Alexander's Ragtime Band" on his little tin balls with his own long leather dong! (*To* ANNABELLE) Did you know I was a happily married man?

ANNABELLE   It doesn't bother me if it doesn't bother you.

ANGUS   Black coffee, please! Can we have some black coffee, please?

DYLAN   To Caitlin. My Caitlin. I love Caitlin. Oh, God. She's as pretty as the princess on top of the Christmas tree. She was a very extraordinary dancer. I ruined her career. She was a top model—for Augustus John. She draws very well, too. She writes better than I do. Wait. I have a letter. (*Fumbling through his pockets*) I lost it. I must have left it somewhere. I destroyed her selfishly. I took this beautiful, brilliant woman and I wiped her out! I used her. I use people, Angus. I'm a Communist! I'm a Puritan! I'm a drunk! And I'm a heterosexual!

MATTOCK   And you're a dirty liar. Sit down, Dylan.

DYLAN   I'll punch the daylights out of any man here that says a kind word about me! (*Pinches* MEG *again*) Toot! Toot!

ANGUS   Dylan, Jesus! Meg, I don't know what to say.

DYLAN   My father is a schoolmaster and a very proper soul—appalled by my incredibly gauche behavior. And he can't make sense of my poems, besides. He likes Wordsworth. He thinks the world is crazy to listen to me. I think he's maybe right. I think—I have to pee now. Where's my fly? Where'd my fly fly? My fly flew the coop.

BARTENDER   (*Rushes over, grabs* DYLAN)   Hold it! Hold it! You just go over there in the corner there where you see the sign that says "Men." You can't do things like that in the middle of the room. There's a room for that that says "Men." You go over there now where you see "Men."

DYLAN

MATTOCK   Come on, Dylan. I'll help you.
(He takes his crutches)

DYLAN *(Helping MATTOCK)*   Would you, Mattock? Will you help me?

ANGUS *(Rising)*   I'll help you too, Dylan. We'll all help you. *(To MATTOCK)* Where were you before you got here?

MATTOCK   Everywhere. He doesn't know how to drink.
(BRINNIN walks on—stands aghast—unobserved)

DYLAN   Liquor is my cross! Liquor is my curse! I am a man with my pinky finger caught in a beer bottle. I can't write like this, Mattock. Can you when you're like this? Oh! I've betrayed the good gift, the good gift! Oh! Hello, John. What's happening?

BRINNIN   Good God! Angus, I'll kill you. Look at him. Do you all know what time it is? It's ten past eight. In twenty minutes he steps out on stage to thunderous applause and goes head first into the orchestra pit.

ANGUS   We're helping him to the men's room first.

DYLAN   Oh, John Malcolm Brinnin. Call it off! I can't! I can't!

BRINNIN   You have to! You've got to try.

DYLAN   You're ten years too late. I can't come through. I'm through.

BRINNIN   Dylan, please. For me! For Caitlin!

DYLAN   At last you know what you invited to America. All right. I'll try. For Caitlin. Pope Eliot's world can end with a whimper, mine's gonna end with one hell of a bang!
(He's helped off by MATTOCK)

ANGUS   You can't put that man up on the podium.

BRINNIN   I can't cancel it! That's my decision.

ANGUS   You'll destroy him!

BRINNIN   Not before you will. I got a letter from his wife today. She doesn't have money for food.

ANGUS   If he goes on and is a flop?

BRINNIN   If he fails to show, the tour's over anyway. Go pour cold water on him. I'll get some black coffee. Here's some. *(To the* WAITER) Thank you.
*(*ANGUS *exits into the men's room)*

MEG   Hello, John.

BRINNIN   Would you hail us a cab, Meg, please?

MEG *(Nods)*   I'll get my coat.

ANNABELLE   How do you do, Mr. Brinnin? I hope he—

BRINNIN   I hope so, too. Besides everything else, I'll probably be out of a job. I need a drink. No. My God, no. Never mind.

35

ANNABELLE   I see a cab! I'll get it! Taxi! Yoohoo!
(*She exits*)

ANGUS (*Rushes out of the men's room*)   Dylan's choking
to death in there. He says he can't breathe and he's spitting blood. We'll pick up my doctor en route. Call him.
Levinson. Fifty-seventh Street. I don't think it's too serious. No food.

BRINNIN   Levinson. Levinson.
(*Rushes off to the phone*)

BYSTANDER (*To* MEG)   Who's the guy the fuss is all
about?

MEG   Oedipus Rex. He killed his father and married his
mother.

BYSTANDER   Jesus!
(*He exits leaving* MEG *alone. There is a moment of
silence as* MEG *picks up her purse, looks over the
table of empty glasses. She shakes her head*)

MEG   And what a goddam waste!
(*The lights go down; then come up on the Ninety-
second Street Y.M.H.A. Kaufmann Concert Hall.
On stage. In the wings. A feeling of ropes and cur-
tains.* BRINNIN *runs on*)

BRINNIN   Dylan? I've just introduced him to the audience.
Where is he?

STAGE MANAGER (*With a clipboard in hand*)   He hasn't
walked through that stage door yet.

36

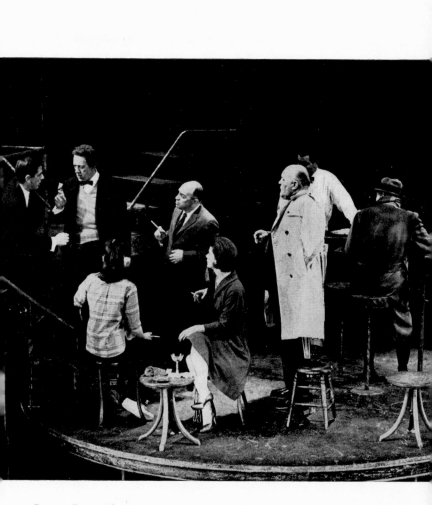

James Ray, Alec Guinness, Jenny O'Hara, Martin Garner, Barbara Berjer, Gordon B. Clarke, Paul Larson, and Ernest Graves, as BRINNIN, DYLAN, ANNABELLE, ANGUS, MEG, MATTOCK, BARTENDER, and BYSTANDER.

BRINNIN But he was right behind me in the cab.

STAGE MANAGER You don't suppose he thought it was **the** Y.M.C.A. do you?

BRINNIN What are we going to do?

STAGE MANAGER I don't know. We're forty-five minutes late now. You're in charge.

BRINNIN Angus!

STAGE MANAGER What do you mean?

BRINNIN They stopped off to see a doctor.

STAGE MANAGER Is he sick?

BRINNIN Drunk! Angus swore it wouldn't take more than five minutes.

STAGE MANAGER What do you want to do?

BRINNIN Die!

STAGE MANAGER You shouldn't have let him out of your sight.

BRINNIN I shouldn't have taken this job. I'm a poet. I'm not an entrepreneur!

STAGE MANAGER Did you just tell that audience "and here he is"?

37

BRINNIN "And here he is, Mr. Dylan Thomas." Applause. Pause. Nothing!

STAGE MANAGER Have you got a whole tour yet ahead of you?

BRINNIN It depends on tonight. It depends on whether or not he can come through. It's the result board we worship, right? Monster or freak, idiot or genius. What have you done for us tonight? That's what they say in the marketplace. That's what the lady says on her back in bed. That's what the gentleman says after he shakes your hand. Come through or be damned!

STAGE MANAGER Why don't you call it off?

BRINNIN No! I won't. I won't.

ANGUS (*Enters*) He's here. We hit every red light en route.
(MATTOCK *and* ANNABELLE *enter, holding* DYLAN, *who's coughing, doubled up.*)

BRINNIN (*To* DYLAN) You're introduced.

ANGUS He'll never make it.

BRINNIN Dylan? You're on.

ANGUS I'm going out there and cop out for him.

BRINNIN You're doing nothing of the kind, Mr. Marius.

DYLAN Beer! Somebody get me some beer.

BRINNIN Dylan, there's hot coffee for you. There isn't any beer.

ANNABELLE No, I got him some beer. He asked me to in the cab.

DYLAN Bless you, my true blue Annabella-balla-boola-boola!

BRINNIN (*Reluctantly agreeing with* ANGUS) I'll call it off. What's the sense?

DYLAN No. I'm fine. I can do it. Where's my poems? (MATTOCK *hands them to him*) Thank you. Where's the podium? Point me toward the damn thing.

BRINNIN Dylan, forget it. Nothing's that important.

DYLAN No, I—I'll be all right if I can reach the podium. I'll be brilliant, I promise. (BRINNIN *shakes his head, starts on to the stage.* DYLAN, *with sudden belligerence, grabs* BRINNIN'S *arm*) John, damn you, if you step out there, I'll be right alongside you and you're going to look like a bloody ass.

BRINNIN Dylan, you can't possibly—

DYLAN (*Gently*) Relax, John. You look harried and care-worn.
    (*He pats him on the back and steps out onto the stage*)

ANGUS Stop him.

39

BRINNIN It's too late now.

> (DYLAN *walks out onto the stage toward the podium to a thunderous applause on the loudspeaker. Silence*)

DYLAN (*Hesitantly, faltering*) For my first—for my—for my first poem I should like to read a poem whose title is its first line. "In My Craft or Sullen Art." (*And then in full vigor*)
"In my craft or sullen art
Exercised in the still night
When only the moon rages
And the lovers lie abed
With all their griefs in their arms,
I labour by singing light
Not for ambition or bread
Or the strut and trade of charms
On the ivory stages
But for the common wages
Of their most secret heart.

"Not for the proud man apart
From the raging moon I write
On these spindrift pages
Nor for the towering dead
With their nightingales and psalms
But for the lovers, their arms
Round the griefs of the ages,
Who pay no praise or wages
Nor heed my craft or art."

> (*There is great applause.* DYLAN *mouths* "Thank you, thank you, thank you very much." *The lights*

go down; then come up on a Park Avenue apart-
ment, later that night. By projection, a kaleidoscope
of colorful shapes like a rainbow in motion conveys
the effect of a crowded cocktail party. There is sing-
ing heard offstage: "Oh, you take the high road and
I'll take the low road and I'll be in Scotland afore
you," etc.)

ANNABELLE (*To* MEG)   Where are you going?

MEG   Home.

ANNABELLE   But we're all off to bar-hopping later.

MEG   You be bar-hopping. There's very little Welsh rabbit
in me.

ANNABELLE   Isn't he everything you ever expected a poet
to be?
    (*She exits as* ANGUS *enters*)

MEG (*To* ANGUS)   Good night, Angus.

ANGUS   What a success! They ate him up tonight!

MEG   It's the biggest last-minute recovery act since 1932.
    (*As* ANGUS *exits,* BRINNIN *enters*)

BRINNIN   You going, Meg?

MEG   Yes, John. Congratulations.

BRINNIN   Did you have a chance to talk to Dylan?

MEG   No. He's been far too busy racing about blowing down the dickies of every girl at the brawl.

BRINNIN   He's not like that all the time.

MEG   I'm sure not. He must sleep sometime.

BRINNIN   Come. I'll get you a cab.

MEG   No, thanks.

DYLAN (*Popping on followed by* ANNABELLE)   Where is Katherine Anne Porter? (*He finds* MISS PORTER *seated in a chair with her hat on, the image of propriety*) Ah, I see her now! You can't escape a Welshman's wonder! Katherine Anne Porter, I love your short stories. *Pale Horse, Pale Rider!* Just for that, I shall lift you up to the stars where you belong.
    (*He proceeds to lift her up onto his shoulders*)

ANGUS   Dylan! My God!

MISS PORTER   Put me down, Dylan Thomas! You're drunk!

DYLAN   Katherine Anne Porter, you're head and shoulders over every other woman writer in the world.

MISS PORTER   Put me down!

ANGUS   Dylan, that's Katherine Anne Porter!

DYLAN   Piggyback! Off we go from room to room! Duck! Low bridge!

(*As* DYLAN *carries her away*)

MISS PORTER   Help! Help!

MEG   My sentiments precisely.
(*She exits*)

ANNABELLE   Hey! Me next! Me next! Dylan!
(*She runs out after* DYLAN)

ANGUS (*To* BRINNIN)   John, my God—come quick. We've
got to rescue Katherine Anne.

BRINNIN (*Asprawl on a chair, laughing weakly*)   You
rescue her, Angus! I'm fresh out of white chargers.

ANGUS   Are you just going to sit there and laugh?

BRINNIN   Uh-huh.

ANGUS   Well, somebody has to help Katherine Anne.

BRINNIN (*Lifting his glass on high*)   It's a Marx Brothers'
movie, Angus. It's Salvador Dali stepping off the canvas.
(ANGUS *goes—fussy and furious*) And all over the aca-
demic literary world, hair'll be let down this year, and
heels will kick, and dresses'll catch in zippers, and banana
peels shall strew the sidewalks, and pins shall pop bal-
loons and beer shall drop from clouds and people shall
cry because we die and laugh because we're born and
you and I, Angus Marius, you sick-ophant, shall have
the book dust blasted off us and be like kids again. Dear
God, I have to call Boston—and I'm potted.

43

(ANNABELLE *re-enters carrying* DYLAN, *piggyback, amid a collegiate crowd*)

ALL (*Sing lustily*)
New York, New York's a hell of a town.
The Bronx is up and the Battery's down.
Two-Four-Six-Eight
Who do we appreciate?
Dylan! Dylan!
>(*The lights go down; the fish net drops and the next scene plays before it. As the lights go up a transatlantic telephone call is in progress, between* DYLAN *and* CAITLIN. *The quality of the scene is one of shouting*)

CAITLIN (*On the telephone*) My husband is in America. Why are you the London operator? What? Are you deliberately whispering? I can't make head or tail out of your excuses. I have to come all the way down here to the Post Office for this call, mind you, and then the quality of your instruments is scarcely worth the trouble, is it? Hello? Hello? Who's that?

DYLAN Hello? Cat?

CAITLIN Dylan? Dylan?

DYLAN I can hear the Atlantic Ocean. Where are *you?*

CAITLIN What? Hello?

DYLAN Hello! We're a sensation! I get tremendous ad-lib laughs between poems and a huge ovation. Bookings have been flooding in. I played Brooklyn. I'm going to Chicago. We wind up at Harvard on the eleventh. Hello?

CAITLIN   How did it go?

DYLAN   I love you. Can you hear me?

CAITLIN   Where are you tonight, you bloody cheat?

DYLAN   How are Colm and Aeron and Llewellyn? What?

CAITLIN   Tuition! The *tuition money*, Dylan!

DYLAN   Yes. Llewellyn's school tuition. Didn't we pay that?

CAITLIN   We didn't *pay* it. Have you *got* it?

DYLAN   My God, we forgot to—will they wait?

CAITLIN   You mustn't disappoint him again. They've threatened to toss him out on his ear. Send it! Good-bye. Let's not spend it all on the telephone. Get off the phone.

DYLAN   What the hell are you saying? Talk up. How's my father?

CAITLIN   I said this is costing us a fortune.

DYLAN   It is. If you'd listen to the questions and answer them one at a time, it would take half the time and cost us half the fortune!

45

CAITLIN What?

DYLAN Oh, Christ!

CAITLIN I haven't any money, either.

DYLAN Write me. Write me. Write me.

CAITLIN You might ask after your father's health, in the name of God.

DYLAN I *did!*

CAITLIN Are you a bloody flop there? Or are you too drunk to tell?

DYLAN Do you know what this phone call is costing us? Have you no sense of the value of money?

CAITLIN You know what the trouble with our lives is—it's a bad connection from a terribly long distance.

DYLAN No good. I can't hear you if you persist in mumbling.

CAITLIN Dylan?

DYLAN Good night!
(*He hangs up*)

CAITLIN Money! Money! Money! I love you, Dylan. Oh, go to hell!
(*She hangs up. The lights go down, the fish net lifts, the lights come up, revealing a darkened child's*

bedroom in a house in Harvard Square. BRINNIN
opens the door—party sounds are heard offstage)

BRINNIN   Dylan? Dylan? I can't see coming out of the
light. Are you in here?

DYLAN   Ssh. Talk softly. I'm over here. By the boy's crib.

BRINNIN   But Dylan, everybody's out there especially to
meet you. Dick and Betty invited the entire faculty.

DYLAN   How'd I do tonight, entrepreneur?

BRINNIN   You put Harvard College in your pocket.

DYLAN   A handsome sum, indeed.

BRINNIN   Did you remember to mail Llewellyn's school
tuition money?

DYLAN   Yes. Yes.

BRINNIN   No, Dylan, look in your pockets. The blue envelope that I made out and stamped for you.

DYLAN   A blue envelope. I carried it in front of my nose
all day yesterday. John, he's been humiliated before
when I've forgotten or didn't have it. I wouldn't let that
happen again. Of course, I mailed it.

BRINNIN   Because if it didn't go out yesterday, they'll toss
him out of school.

DYLAN   I know. I know. Just because Cat wrote you not to trust me, Brinnin, is no reason to play den mother. I mailed the bloody blue envelope. Good enough?

BRINNIN   I'm sorry. Your being an hour late to your M.I.T. reading's got me a little edgy. But that couldn't be helped. If you overslept, you overslept. Sorry. Come on back to the party.

DYLAN   Not yet. Not yet.

BRINNIN   I brought your drink.

DYLAN   I don't want it. Set it down someplace.

BRINNIN   I thought you wanted to see the midnight show at the Old Howard.

DYLAN   Shame on you.

BRINNIN   The party's in your honor out there, you know.

DYLAN   I'm sure it is. Tell them in there I'm asleep. Or drunk. Or dizzy. Or dead. I'm not up to having my trouser cuffs kissed tonight. (*He looks at the boy asleep*) He reminds me of Llewellyn and Colm, my boys. My poor boys. He reminds me of me when I was a boy. He's afraid of the dark. Sit down. It's nice here.

BRINNIN   How'd you get in here.

DYLAN   I heard him. Crying. Nothing worth bothering his parents with. We had a bit of a talk and a laugh or two. Facts of life and a dirty joke.

BRINNIN   How old is he?

DYLAN   Three. The age of wisdom. To believe in fairies and to be not quite yet toilet-trained. He asked me to tell him a bedtime story. I gave my best reading in weeks. I wish you'd been here.

BRINNIN (*Smiling*)   What poem did you read, Dylan, to a three-year-old boy?

DYLAN   Not one of my own. But one of my favorite poems and the story of my life.
" 'Baa, baa, black sheep!
Have you any wool?'
'Yes, sir. Yes, sir. Three bags full!
One for my master
One for my dame
And one for the little boy who lives down the lane.' "

BRINNIN   Is that your life story, Dylan?

DYLAN   Yes. Every blessed word of it! "Baa, baa, black sheep" refers, of course, to me, who am the black sheep of my family, mankind—the "Baa, baa," is the comment, point of view—then, "Have you any wool?" is the request life makes of poets—Have you any long rainbow strands of woolly thoughts to be woven into the dense and lovely fabric of poems which are the ferventest of prayers by which men praise God and this, his slap-dash Eden, continually lost and found and lost, alas. To which I answer up, very polite and eager, "Yes, sir. Yes sir"—that's being affirmative, positive—"Three bags full"

—that's bragging—'s probably only two bags or a bag and a half, of talent to spend, of wit to squander, of love to give. And who to, to give it? Why, the answer's almost immediate. "One for my master"—God. "One for my dame"—Cat. The best-looking "dame" I know. "And one for the little boy who lives—down the lane." That's myself from long-away once-upon days. The lane is memory, the winded, winding, wound-up, wounded, wondrous, winning thing. The bag for myself is probably the one I don't have. The brag bag. But then in its place the story offers me consolation in that there's no end to it. The little boy lives. Lives. Lives. He never has to die. He may be a black sheep and all that but he gives everything he's got to give, away to others to serve their need—so he gets to live forever for it—in his poems, John, in his bag of poems.

BRINNIN I never knew the specific meaning of that verse before.

DYLAN Oh, yes. That's what it's about. Now listen and you'll see how clear it is when you're in the know.
" 'Baa baa, black sheep!
Have you any wool?'
'Yes, sir. Yes, sir. Three bags full!
One for my master
One for my dame
And one for the little boy who *lives*
        (*Pause*)
Down the lane.' "
Huh. A curious thing. You know? Here I am, truly as if I had finally arrived at the height of my gift, with all

the craft at my finger tips, knowing exactly what to do, to say exactly what's to be said, just as I seem to have run out of the drive to say it. I'll tell you what that's like. That's like all the good fairies around the cradle and the one malevolent hag that levels the crooked finger that curdles the cream of the blessings—that one malevolent hag—that cries across my bunting, "If this child is going to grow up, this child is going to grow old! And sing no more!" And it fills me with rage. It fills me with rage.

(The lights go down; in the dark:)

LOUDSPEAKER —Old Howard Theater, the home of family entertainment whose motto is "Anything can happen," proudly presents its star attraction and her world-renowned, inspiring, exotic dance: Miss Thelma Wonderland!

(A pink spot shines on a gold-tasseled, split, velvet curtain as the overly introduced MISS WONDERLAND enters and begins to strip to the heavy downbeat of an unmistakable burlesque drum. Off stage an altercation is heard of loud voices and scuffling. Among them DYLAN's voice, drunk. MISS WONDERLAND continues her strip but glances nervously off stage. Suddenly DYLAN barges out drunkenly onto the stage beside her. BRINNIN, edging out after him, tugs his sleeve. MISS WONDERLAND turns and sees both. She screams and grabs the curtain to cover herself. The dialogue overlaps)

DYLAN My dear child, I won't hurt you.

BRINNIN Dylan, please.

MISS WONDERLAND   Tell Max to get this drunken bum off my stage!

DYLAN   A thing of beauty is a joy forever! Why isn't your name Joy Forever?

STAGEHAND (*Entering*)   Okay, okay! Take it easy, Miss Wonderland. Come on, my friend. Let's move it.

DYLAN (*To* STAGEHAND)   Will you be my friend?

BRINNIN   Please, you can't treat him like a common—
(*A blue envelope falls out of* DYLAN'S *pocket—* BRINNIN *picks it up*)

STAGEHAND (*To* BRINNIN)   You, too, Charley. Off the stage!

BRINNIN (*Recognizing the envelope*)   Dylan, Llewellyn's tuition money! You didn't send it!

DYLAN (*Merrily oblivious*)   Thelma, take it off! I'm mad as birds for you! Thelma! I'm reading at Radcliffe tomorrow.
(*He's bum-rushed off.* BRINNIN, *apologetic, follows, wiping his brow with a handkerchief*)

LOUDSPEAKER   And now, Miss Wonderland will continue her world-renowned, inspiring, exotic dance—alone.
(*A bump. A grind. The lights die to a descending sour trumpet, which in the dark becomes the profound double-bass note of an ocean liner. The lights rise to reveal* DYLAN *in the upper berth of a very*

small ship's cabin. The place is strewn with luggage, flowers, baskets of fruit, and champagne buckets. An EPISCOPALIAN MINISTER, *his collar on, reaches up to* DYLAN *and shakes his hand*)

MINISTER   How do you do. I'm the Reverend Breathwhite. I'm your shipmate for the voyage.

DYLAN (*Warmly*)   My deepest deepest sympathies. Angus, pour a little holy water for this man of the burning cloth.

ANGUS (*Appearing from around the bunk as if out of nowhere*)   I arise from the lamp in a puff of smoke—you rubbed, sir? My name is Genie! Once I had a light brown hair but no longer. Today I am bald and forthright. This is a terrific sailing party. Have you met any of the girls, Reverend? They're out in the companionway, all potential converts. Come with me.
      (ANNABELLE *squeezes past* ANGUS *and the* MINISTER *as they exit. She is dressed in black with a veil, like a widow*)

ANNABELLE   Dylan! Alas. 'Tis parting time.

DYLAN   My God, Annabelle—you're in weeds—this isn't the *Titanic*.

ANNABELLE   You'll never come back. I have a feeling.

DYLAN   I'll be back, my dear, next year.

ANNABELLE   Christmas in New York?

DYLAN   I'll try. I'll try.

ANNABELLE   She won't let you out of the house.

DYLAN   Now, now. She has prior rights.

ANNABELLE   I never had it so good.

DYLAN   Nor I. Nor any man on earth. You're just a reckless child, Annabelle. You don't know what to do with it all.

BRINNIN   Annabelle, your father is out in the companionway and he wants to see you. He says farewell to you, Dylan, but he says it's too hot and crowded in here so he's staying out there—talking to Meg.

DYLAN   Meg? Is she here? Meg! My bosom pal!

ANNABELLE   I'll be back for a kiss good-bye.

DYLAN   Oh, Annabelle, Annabelle. Squeeze my hand and go at once. Don't look back.

ANNABELLE   All right. Squeeze!
       (*She goes*)

DYLAN   John, I may be in love with that foolish girl.

BRINNIN   Annabelle?

DYLAN   I don't know. I'm not sure. I love Caitlin. But I love Annabelle, too. I love them all. I love women. I love men. I love you. I love my shipmate. He's got his collar on backwards but then I'm a careless dresser myself. I love boats and bottles and Wales and America. I want to come back here.

BRINNIN   You will—someday.

DYLAN (*Suddenly briskly*)   Will you promise to arrange it for next year?

BRINNIN   Look, I've got to go over these figures with you. I just spent two weeks making out all your expenses and earnings. You have to know all this for tax purposes.

DYLAN   Not now, John. That's really bully of you. Stick it in my bag there and refill my glass.

BRINNIN   I slaved over this, Dylan. I'm not an accountant, I'm a poet. Don't you want to hear what you earned?

DYLAN   Why? I spent it all already.

BRINNIN   You what? You haven't. You couldn't have.

DYLAN   I don't know how. It just seemed to go. Every night. All those people. I haven't a nickel left. Cat'll kill me. I may throw myself to the fishes before I reach Wales. Facing Llewellyn's what destroys me. How could I have let him down? I love him so. Here he was humiliated to tears being tossed out of school for no money and here I was living it up, lapping it up and the bloody money sitting in my pocket. Oh, Johnny Brinnin, I'm such a failure as a human being that it's something fierce.

BRINNIN   There's three hundred dollars left.

55

DYLAN   No. It's all gone. I looked this morning when I packed. Oh, God!

BRINNIN   There's three hundred dollars. I kept it from you. It's in your shaving kit all rolled up. It was to have been kind of a secret bonus, but I guess it's your whole net profit now.

DYLAN   (*Suddenly furious*)   Didn't you trust me, goddam it?

BRINNIN   No, Dylan, I didn't!

DYLAN   (*Pause*)   Thank God! My dear friend. Forever, Brinnin. Get me back. I have to come back. You're my man in America.

BRINNIN   I don't think you should too soon. It's been a brilliant tour, but for you personally—

DYLAN   I'll write here, next time. I'll hang onto the money. It'll be different!

BRINNIN   I may visit you in Wales in the fall. We'll talk about it then.

DYLAN   You'll meet Caitlin. She'll love you. Yes, come to Wales! You must!
        (MEG *steps in*)

MEG   Good-bye, Dylan.

DYLAN   Meg. I didn't really think you'd come to see me off.

BRINNIN   There's the whistle. I better start moving some
of the crowd outside off or they'll be sailing with you.
(BRINNIN *exits*)

MEG   Angus says there's several bottles of Scotch in the
paper bag in the corner.

DYLAN   You hate him for doing that.

MEG   I guess he figures if he doesn't buy it for you, you'll
spend your own money on it.

DYLAN   You disapprove of me.

MEG   I do, Dylan.

DYLAN   Huh. What can I be? I've been me for so long
now. There's no turning around.

MEG   I could turn you around.

DYLAN   Would you?

MEG   Would you let me?

DYLAN   When I come back, we must have lunch. Work
on Angus and John. Don't let them forget me. Kiss me
good-bye, as if you meant it.

MEG   Wrong girl.

DYLAN   My dear Meg, a sailing party is a time for
whoopee.

MEG Then where are you always sailing, Dylan?

LOUDSPEAKER All visitors ashore. All visitors ashore.
     (*As* MEG *exits and* BRINNIN *and* MATTOCK *push past
     her into the cabin*)

MATTOCK (*On a cane now*) So long, Dylan, you tipsy
     tough. This damn stick takes forever to carry me.

DYLAN Lose weight!

MATTOCK You, too, you filthy dog! And write!
     (MATTOCK *exits, leaving* DYLAN *and* BRINNIN *alone*)

DYLAN Well, John Malcolm Brinnin. My host. Say the
     good word.

BRINNIN Baa, baa, black sheep.

DYLAN You may pass. Favor, favor. Would you hand me
     that paper bag in the corner like a good friend?

BRINNIN Sure. What's in it?

DYLAN Nibbles. Sweets. Drops, I think.

BRINNIN Dylan, I'll get you back here someday.

DYLAN Next year. Bless you. Go on! Go on! (*Boat whistle.*
     JOHN *goes. The* MINISTER *comes in, his collar askew,
     hair a little wild, bewildered.* DYLAN *takes a bottle out
     of his paper bag—opens it and drinks deep. The* MINISTER
     watches him aghast. DYLAN *catches his eye and cries:*)
     God bless America!

(The lights go down. The boat horn booms in the dark, establishing the return of DYLAN *to Wales. The fish net drops and fades through to the ocean sounds, the beach in Wales, the spiles, the stairs, the boathouse. It is evening. There is a reddish light. Stars appear in the course of the scene.* DYLAN *is being helped up the stairs by* CAITLIN, *who has brought him back from the station.* DYLAN *is dog-tired, beery)*

DYLAN   I'm dying! I can't keep it up.

CAITLIN   You're not dying!

DYLAN   I can't keep it up. I'm seasick. Plane sick. Train sick. Brain sick.

CAITLIN   You're going to bed now. You'll survive.

DYLAN   I was brilliant! They loved me! The whole continent loves me. I was terrific! I really was, Cat! I was terribly good. And they, they, they loved me!

CAITLIN   Everyone loves you, Dylan!

DYLAN   Not enough!

CAITLIN   Come. One step. Take another. One more step. Up, up.

DYLAN   Omaha! In Daytona! It's an immense country. Since they killed the Indians—you don't see any Indians —they've got nothing but space over there. You should

59

see what posh cars American poets drive. Brinnin has a Studebaker. It's only two years old. Isn't that posh?

CAITLIN Put your arm around my shoulder!

DYLAN Buildings as tall as Babel! We're going to be rich, Cat. We're going to pay all our debts and have luxuries and necessities—just like everybody.

CAITLIN With what, Dylan? You spent it all but three hundred dollars.

DYLAN Doesn't matter. I'm a man of letters. I can have it anytime I want it again. They worship me. They saved my empty beer bottles to donate to museums. I must be very great. You know that?

CAITLIN I know it, Dylan. Do you?

DYLAN I have to laugh. I met the critics and I had them completely bamboozled. All I did was keep saying hum, hum, and puffing this—cigar! As big as a stevedore's dingus! One compared me to Shakespeare! And Keats! Campuses turned out in my honor! The applause at those readings. It loved me. I tell you, I fornicated an entire nation with the sound of my voice!

CAITLIN You're never going back. Never again.

DYLAN I am! For the money. The freedom of the money. Free of my debts. Drowned in the money. So I can concentrate, sit, sit—that's why I'm ready, anxious, desperate, Jesus, Caitlin, poetry!

CAITLIN They've spoiled you rotten—you're dissipated and flabby and fat and sick to the soul! Listen to you. You egotist!

DYLAN I'm spitting blood. I had two blackouts. I've been running, running. I'm so tired.

CAITLIN Come. You're going to bed now.

DYLAN To have sex!

CAITLIN To sleep! Didn't you have enough sex in America, enough liquor, enough adulation? What do you have to be—the bloody Pope, Dylan?

DYLAN Yes! You don't understand. I'm as famous as God! They all want to meet you. I told them all how you're as pretty as the princess on top of the Christmas tree. Listen, forgive me about not writing so often—I was—

CAITLIN Listen to me! You're never going back to America. They've *had* you and you've *had* them!

DYLAN What do you mean?

CAITLIN Stop for one minute, Dylan—stop. Don't you know what you've been through?
    (*A pause*)

DYLAN (*Softly*) Yes, I do. It's no good for me. Success will kill me. I don't want to die! I'm so lonely. Oh, God, Cat—I'm so lonely. Don't let me go back, Cat. Don't let me go.

(She holds him tightly to her. She kisses his head. He cries, shaken. She closes her eyes and takes a deep breath. The sound of the ocean rolling in on the beach washes over the moment. The stars of Wales glitter in the night. As the fish-net curtain slowly drops and the scene dissolves to darkness)

CURTAIN

Act Two

ACT II

A chain of telephone calls. As each pool of light rises, the character speaks. The calls are disconnected and in quick sequence.

BRINNIN   Augus? John Brinnin. I just got back from Wales. Sit down.

AUGUS   (*As he sits*)   Both of them are coming? Good luck to America!

MEG   Angus, I did promise to have lunch with him but I'm certainly not going to have lunch with him with his wife here. I don't care what you say Dylan expects.

MATTOCK   Brinnin, wait'll I adjust the phone here. I broke my arm. Look, I'm delighted to have Dylan again but I want your word, John, that he shows up this time. By the time he showed up last time, my classes were graduated.

ANNABELLE   Jesus, I've made a terrible mistake, Augus. I never thought he'd come back. I got married.

ANGUS   You heard me. Angus Marius. I want to reserve three tables at the White Horse Tavern for October tenth. I know you don't reserve tables but it's a party

65

for Dylan! Right. Didn't we pay for the glassware? This is entirely different. His wife'll be with him.

CAITLIN Mrs. Dylan Thomas here. Who is this? *Time* magazine? What do you want? We just walked through the door of our hotel. He's lying down and can't be disturbed. What do *I* think of you? I think you're all too bloody pleasant and I don't trust you as far as I can throw you. And if I had my way, we wouldn't be here.

ANGUS (*Party noises behind him*) Brinnin? How's your terrible cold? Angus. I'm calling you from the White Horse Tavern. It's a wonderful party, a wonderful party. Cat is just enjoying herself immensely. But is Dylan with you? Then I've lost him.

DYLAN (*In a phone booth*) Meg? This is Dylan Thomas. I'm back in America and you're in the phonebook! Would you like to have lunch with me? Now! It's only four o'clock in the morning. Look, I'm going to be very sick. If Cat sees me, she'll get scared and go home. I've still got half a bottle of booze to go. I'm at the corner of Bleecker and Sixth Avenue. It's starting to rain. Come, pick me up for lunch.

    (*The lights go down. Thunder is heard in the dark. The lights rise on* MEG'S *bathroom in a cold-water flat. The tub is practical. She leads* DYLAN *in, who is bloody, dirty, drunk and babbling. Proceeds to take his clothes off, run the water, etc.*)

DYLAN The sky's divorced! The weather's go boom. What are we doing? Who am I?

MEG   We're taking off your clothes, Dylan. You're little boy lost.

DYLAN   I hear water running.

MEG   We're about to take a tub. As I haven't got a shower. You seem to have lain in a muddy gutter and you've evidently been in a fist fight. No, leave your shorts on. Arm around my shoulder and don't you dare touch my breasts.

DYLAN   'Pologize. Is it cold?

MEG   Ice cold.

DYLAN   Wonderful! (*Gets in*) Jesus God, it's ice cold! Are you out of your bloody mind? Don't splash! Oh, no! Oh, no. I've still got my shorts on here. What a feeling! (*She laughs*) I bet nobody in his right mind loves you.

MEG   Nobody in his right mind interests me.

DYLAN   Brrr. No beaux, successful or otherwise?

MEG   I overprune my garden, sir—nothing grows in it.

DYLAN   I didn't go to college. You'll have to explain that.

MEG   Well, I'll tell you how it is: Basketball giants pick me up for the theater at eight and are whittled to pygmies by eight-fifteen. Sharp repartee. At eight twenty-five, we reach the theater, and I help them out of the cab. By intermission time I hold them in my arms like dolls. Drinks after the show finds them further reduced to hand puppets; they are in the palm of the hand they'd like to hold. At last, what brings me home and begs me to let it come in for coffee and monkeyshines is microscopic and therefore biologically unfitted to giving me anything more than a bad headcold.

DYLAN   Oh you're "a love." Why didn't you leave me in the gutter where you found me?

MEG   I'm a Girl Scout and an English major.

DYLAN   Nonsense. You're at least a Brigadier. Have you no daddy or mummy?

MEG   A mummy. My daddy died of a very bad case of cheap rye. People whom liquor melts no longer shock me. But I never seem to be able to walk fast in the opposite direction. I'm patriotic for drunks.

DYLAN   Say, you wouldn't like to go to bed with a wild Welsh poet, would you?

MEG   I don't think so.

DYLAN   I thought not. (*A phone rings*) Whoops! I'm not here whoever that is.

MEG   Don't splash about.

DYLAN   Jesus, you don't think it's Caitlin, do you?

MEG   That's life. Here's a towel.
    (*She goes out.* DYLAN *gets out of tub and dries off*)

DYLAN   This girl has got to go. There's a vicious draft in here. (*He looks in the mirror*) Oh, Dylan, you foul-haired boy, look at you—you're all wet, as usual. (*He puts on her robe. Looks down at himself*) Charley's aunt. (MEG *returns*) Cat? Was it Cat?

MEG   Angus. He's going to call Cat and tell her you're conked out at his place, sleeping it off.

DYLAN   Good. No sense dropping our tobacco butts in good liquor. No point mentioning I am here alone with you without my clothes on in a private room at an ungodly hour. What do you suppose I'm hinting at? I suppose I'm hinting at an orgy and I don't even feel like an orgy. I wouldn't know what to do with an orgy if I had one. Still and all, if I don't even hint at it, the sense of waste depresses me for weeks. Thus the clown admits his nose is large.

MEG   Put your duds on and I'll make you some tea.

DYLAN   Tea. That's made with ordinary tap water, isn't it? Can't you make us something antiseptic?

MEG   You can't stay here, Dylan.

DYLAN   Don't you have an apparatus that could open up temporarily for me?

MEG   It's not convertible. Come on, Dylan—I'm a big girl, you're a big boy. And you're married.

DYLAN   Yes. Happily. Happily married.

MEG Three children.

DYLAN You're rejecting me.

MEG Never kill you.

DYLAN I thought you were going to undertake my reformation.

MEG Lost cause. A change of mind.

DYLAN Or a change of heart?

MEG Dress.

DYLAN Without my shorts?

MEG Who'll notice?

DYLAN I hate to tell you.

MEG You're a genius. You've got till tomorrow to plan an explanation. Angus is expecting you at his place tonight.
    (*She starts to go*)

DYLAN Stay. Stay. I'm lousy conversation to myself tonight. You don't have to close your eyes. I can do it under the robe. Houdini, the escape artist.

MEG Why on earth did you come back to America, Dylan?

DYLAN Oh. Why did I come back to America? I've never told this to a living soul but the actual reason is that the British government has built a guided missile site right next to my boathouse in Wales. No, it's quite true. You can't tell if what moves you is the spirit or the blast-off. Impossible conditions to concentrate in. I write "the ground is shaking" and the ground *is* shaking.

MEG Would you be merry at your own funeral, Dylan?

DYLAN Impossible. I'll be late to it. No, I need money. I've just discovered it's the current mode of exchange.

MEG You'll blow every penny you make and you know it.

DYLAN You want to be my business manager?

MEG Isn't John?

DYLAN Only for the tour.

MEG Cat'd hit the roof. You *are* Houdini, Dylan. The escape artist.

DYLAN I'm a highly concentrated person who adores distraction.

MEG Escaping what?

DYLAN You won't let go, will you? Give me a cigarette. Thanks. Escaping. Responsibility, of course. One is always escaping responsibility.

MEG To Cat?

DYLAN To Internal Revenue.

MEG   Please, Dylan. Please be serious. Come down off the rostrum and level with the lady in the balcony. Escaping responsibility to—?

DYLAN   Poetry. I haven't written a bloody word of it in a dog's age. Maybe only one percent of a poet's life is poetry. Ninety-nine percent of the time he's just a human being, but he always knows he's only storing up for that one percent when the magic happens—so he plays pig to supply manure to grow the flowers in. My collected poems are out. Two dollars and fifty cents will buy any acned student of modern verse my total output. But the input I put into that output: my entire life, and when it comes to two dollars and fifty cents, I think I'm overpaid. Because the truth of the matter is I'd have done it for nothing. Still, it's selling like hotcakes. My whole life is selling like hotcakes. If sales keep up over the years, I may make five thousand dollars for my pains.

MEG   Who asked you to be a poet?

DYLAN   Oh, I'm not complaining. It's not bad for something you'd have done for nothing. But I am filled with wonder these days because my collected poems are out and I'm still kicking. Why it's like I've been given a second entire life. And what shall I do with it, having it now to do all over again?

MEG   Dylan, I'll make you a deal.

DYLAN   Good. Go to bed with me and I'll autograph your personal copy of my collected poems. You do have a copy, don't you?

MEG   Yes. I have a copy. Let me tell you what to do with your life, like a schoolmaster, and I'll take ten percent of the satisfaction.

DYLAN   Aren't I living my life correctly, schoolmaster?

MEG   You're not living your life at all.

DYLAN   I'm living it to the hilt!

MEG   Oh, no. Not *your* life. You're only living the poet's life. Stop trying to write poetry. It's not the end of the world. Write plays. Write an opera. Write a film. Write your adventures in America. Cut more records of readings and build yourself an annuity. Let your writing go out and work for you, instead of having to stand up and kill yourself in Des Moines for fifty dollars a show. Do you have any real estate? Stocks? Insurance? You don't live your life, Dylan. You live Riley's life or some image you once got of yourself as the bad-boy genius skidding downhill to a splashy crack-up. And I tell you the magic'll come back if you take a little of the terror of no money and hangovers and sex, unlimited and indiscriminate, and throw those things in the ashcan because *they* are worthless and *you* are valuable. You want to read what they'll write about you after you're dead. But you may not be able to do that. I mean, whoever guaranteed *you* a private resurrection?

DYLAN   Christ.

MEG   If you're plumping for sainthood, you haven't any right to drag Cat and three children down that old path of agony and endurance.

73

DYLAN She drags me, I tell you. She drags me. I'm only living up to how she chooses to see me.

MEG And she chooses to see you how you chose to see yourself twenty years ago. Every damn silly thing that woman says or does is only to match you, outrage for outrage.

DYLAN And I hate that!

MEG Then, how happily married can you be?

DYLAN I lied! I'm not happy. She's not happy. It's not possible to live with her. It gets more impossible every day. I detest the way we are together. And I detest the way I become with her—it's always Punch and Judy, kill and make up. It's always a raging hurricane—you can't live like that. There's no time out for breath, for a life! I'm tired to death of it. And I can't write! I don't know whose fault it is any more—it's both of us now—maybe she'd be better off without me, too. Yes, I love her, I love her—as I love burning coals and bits of colored glass and bright thumbtacks and snakes un-scotched in pits, but I can't walk barefoot on them any longer. My Hindu kidhood's gone. It's gone! Shed like a lizard's skin and I feel newborn and tenderfooted. More so mortal, perhaps. But maybe it's not so terrible a thing as I used to think it would be—a soft berth wall-to-wall in my young old age.

MEG Why don't you try to tell her that?

DYLAN I will. I will.

MEG   One night Mattock said you've a death wish, Dylan.

DYLAN   Baloney. Do you believe I've anything like that, like a death wish?

MEG   When you go on the tour, if you want to talk to me, call me. Reverse the charges.

DYLAN   My unofficial business manager. (*Pause*) I really suppose I better leave.

MEG   Angus doesn't expect you, Dylan. (*Pause*) It's raining out.

DYLAN   I have a birthday coming up. Is this my birthday present?

MEG   There are needs in this world that have nothing to do with love, and marriages that never get recorded in a court house. Happy birthday, Dylan.
    (*And she moves towards him; the lights go down. They go up on the Metropolitan Museum of Art in New York.* CAITLIN *and* BRINNIN *are walking along looking at the pictures, talking*)

CAITLIN   Is this a really good museum?

BRINNIN   The Metropolitan? It's supposed to be one of the best in the world.

CAITLIN   I just asked. I may take singing lessons while I'm in New York.

BRINNIN   I thought you were a dancer, Caitlin.

CAITLIN   Oh, Dylan lost interest in that years ago.

BRINNIN   He asked me to get you two tickets to the ballet Thursday.

CAITLIN   Oh, did he? I may brush up. I may take a few hours of bar work. Do you know a good place?

BRINNIN   I'll look into it.

CAITLIN   When do we leave on the bloody tour?

BRINNIN   You've got almost two weeks. I'm counting on you, Cat. To see that he keeps his dates and gets there sober. I think the tour should be very successful—Dylan's collected poems coming out last month and going so well.

CAITLIN   That's a big help, isn't it? I'm going to keep a diary of the tour so I can sell it to Angus Marius and make us some real money. I can't trust Dylan. He's got a perennial hole in his pocket. I want to get him and the children and myself off to Majorca. We all need a vacation from struggling.

BRINNIN   Look. There's an Augustus John, 1936. "Portrait of a Lady." Listen, why don't we get back down to the main lobby—Dylan and Angus should be turning up any minute—what is it, Caitlin?

CAITLIN   (*Staring at the painting*)   It's me, John. It's me, John. Sixteen years ago. "Dylan Thomas, you'll want to meet Miss Caitlin McNamara." "Good morning, Mr.

Thomas—I've read your poetry. You're all the rage of London now." "I'm the rage of the world, Miss McNamara. But everybody from T. S. Eliot to the chimney sweep calls me Dylan." "Cat's my nickname." "I hate cats, perhaps because I've never had one of my own. Would you like to marry me, Cat?" "When, Dylan?" "This afternoon?" "This afternoon would be fine but as near to late in the day as we can, as I believe in a decent period of courtship." . . . I have that—memorized.

BRINNIN (*Staring at the painting*) Yes, of course it's you.

CAITLIN (*Laughing slightly*) Too late. You didn't know me. I'm like the cliff back in Wales the boathouse backs to, weathered to the edge of collapse. Well, it isn't everyone's youth gets hung in the Metropolitan Museum of Art.

BRINNIN Cat, will you be my friend?

CAITLIN Brinnin, I'll be yours if you'll be mine. Can I count on you when it counts?

BRINNIN I guess that's what I mean by "friend."

CAITLIN And do you know what I mean by "counts"? I mean when all the young predatory American witches flop down in indelicate positions at his feet, are you going to help me beat them off or play "bystander" whose business it suddenly isn't? Because I know who I am. And I'm the life of him. The unhappy, quarreling, domesticated but very necessary life of him. But what I

77

mostly fear is some particular girl in mink or blue jeans or a tailored suit, who'll be the death of him.

BRINNIN   Well, that certainly can't happen if—

CAITLIN   I turn my back and oh, can't it? Dylan's as susceptible to romance as a weeping widow. When he's keyed up like the readings make him, he aches to unwind. His little excursions in London over the years never concerned me, but the bloody man's at a dangerous age in a country of hospitable vampires.

BRINNIN   Cat, I swear to you. I couldn't be more opposed to Dylan's promiscuity if I stood on my head *but*—

CAITLIN   I'm not asking you to stand on your head or on your butt; I'm asking you to lend me a hand or to point out smoke before my house goes up when I turn my back.

BRINNIN   Well, I don't think, Cat, I want to be a tattletale or have to insert myself between Dylan and every little arsonist that turns up for an autograph. Like a chaperone!

CAITLIN   Then *don't ask me to be your friend!*

BRINNIN   Goddam, you're just as bad as he is.

CAITLIN   Of course. Don't you know I'm the woman Dylan'd have been if Dylan had been a woman? That's what I've made of me. And it took three children and the aging years and you'll never know, and nobody, nobody is going to take my place without a fight!

DYLAN

(The lights go down. The time is some weeks later. The lights go up on a darkened hotel room in Texas. Asleep in the bed are DYLAN *and* CAITLIN. *Suddenly* DYLAN *sits bolt upright, grabs the clock and shakes it)*

DYLAN   No! No! It can't be true! My God! *(He turns and shakes* CAITLIN*)* Cat! Cat! Wake up!

CAITLIN *(From under the covers)*   Not if we're still in Texas!

DYLAN   Wake up! The bloody alarm clock has stabbed us in the back.

CAITLIN   We forgot to set it. Jesus, Dylan!

DYLAN   Get up. We've got to get out of here and catch the damn bus to New Orleans by six.

CAITLIN   Where are we, in the name of God?

DYLAN   In Houston.

CAITLIN   No, we were in Houston last week.

DYLAN *(Crossing the room)*   Well, then we're in Austin. They're all alike . . . Shite! I stubbed my toe.

CAITLIN   I hate America!

DYLAN   Will you get out of the bed? It's Tuesday. There's four thousand people at two-fifty a head going to be at the Municipal Auditorium in New Orleans tomorrow night and you're languishing there like you thought you were the Queen of Sheba!

CAITLIN   When I go to hell they're going to make me lie forever on this mattress.

DYLAN   Holy God, my wrist watch isn't going. What does yours say?

CAITLIN   Ten past five.

DYLAN   Great!

CAITLIN   And not ticking.

DYLAN (*With sarcasm*)   Great!

CAITLIN (*Leaping up and running*)   Me first in the bathroom!

DYLAN   You don't have half as much to do in there as I do. Well, hell, I'll start packing and shave in here. Caitlin, why do you have to unpack and spread us out over ten drawers, every time we move into a hotel room?

CAITLIN (*From the other room*)   I have to make a nest, don't I?

DYLAN   In Wales our nest is a sight to behold. I think you do it just to drive me out of my mind. My God, what a beard I've got!

CAITLIN   No sleep! No sleep! We never get any sleep on this bloody tour.

DYLAN Say, this is Tuesday, isn't it?

CAITLIN (*Comes back into room*) Well, last night was Monday night, Dylan—it should be Tuesday.

DYLAN Of course. Of course. It's dark out. (*He's peering out the window*) There's a very peculiar lack of light out today. Like a tropical storm brewing.

CAITLIN It's probably still Monday night.

DYLAN Yes. Yes. I feel as if it were. Oh, now I see. It's dawn. We've tons of time. I can see the sun there rising in the west. Not a bad party, though, they gave us after last night's reading.

CAITLIN If you hadn't thrown that book at me, I would never have thrown the lamp!

DYLAN Worst of it was after we told them all to go to hell and slammed the door, having to go back to borrow the cab fare.

CAITLIN Well, it was that or not have enough for even a bus to New Orleans.

DYLAN And damn Brinnin. Sending us that ridiculous wire, "lest you forget," as if we couldn't get from Dallas to New Orleans without being prodded like pigs every inch of the way.

CAITLIN And he didn't send us a penny to get there with. Dirty Brinnin.

DYLAN Dirty Brinnin. He's kept a shamefully loose grip on this tour is all I can say. I mean he has no right to assume we've money without checking with us.

CAITLIN You should have written him weeks ago.

DYLAN Who's had time to write letters? I'll call him after breakfast. My God, I'm starved. I feel as if I haven't eaten in two days. Tour's nearly over and we haven't a nickel to show for it. Well, it's certainly different this time with you along! It's worse!

CAITLIN I didn't ship two hundred dollars' worth of toys across the Atlantic Ocean!

DYLAN No! You shipped our dirty laundry from Chicago to San Francisco for forty dollars.

CAITLIN I'd do it again. I don't want to go to New Orleans! I want to go home to Wales!

DYLAN Now, you listen to me a minute. Our way of life is a nuthouse. Now, I've seen another way of life in my travels and if you drive me too far, Cat, I'll have to take it. It doesn't include you.

CAITLIN "O, Cat, you're the only girl for me," am I?

DYLAN Love has nothing to do with it. It isn't enough to love you, Cat—I have to support you even if I have to leave you to do it. Now, New Orleans'll make it up to us. There's profit there. Then there's Washington.

CAITLIN I'll go home without you! Who is she?

DYLAN We don't have the fare. Don't you understand? We can't even afford to get out of the country.

CAITLIN I've got such a headache!

DYLAN So have I. Don't fold everything. Just throw it together. Come sit on a suitcase with me. I don't understand how the devil without so much as an added Kleenex, these bags get thicker and thicker every time we pack them up again.

CAITLIN (*Starting to cry*) I don't want to sit on a suitcase.

DYLAN Cat, don't cry. Don't cry, Caitlin. I'll take care of you. I'm at a great turning point of my life. It just isn't so easy to adjust for a fool like me. But I'm trying as hard as I can.

CAITLIN That isn't why I'm crying, Dylan.

DYLAN Why are you crying, Cat? I'm listening, Cat.

CAITLIN Because the sun doesn't rise in the west.
(*He leaps up and looks out the window*)

DYLAN It's gotten darker. You're right. It's Tuesday night.

CAITLIN It must be after six, Dylan. That means we've missed our bus. Good-bye, New Orleans!

DYLAN Not so fast. It's about eight or eight-thirty. We'll wire Brinnin for money and we'll catch a plane. Hello, room service. What time do you have? Eight-thirty. Excellent. Hold the phone, please. I want to order dinner

83

for two. Cat, now what would delight your sea-changed palate? Strictly American cuisine, of course. A deboned, defeathered, defrosted hot dog under glass, washed down with a jumbo-sized paper cup of fermented Coke? Or will it be Chinese food flown in from Pittsburgh?

CAITLIN (*Softly*) Ask room service what day it is, Dylan, while you're at it.

DYLAN (*A long look at her and then into the phone*) Hello, room service? This is *Tuesday* evening, of course . . . It's *Wednesday* evening? It's eight-thirty on Wednesday evening? It can't be that—I've got four thousand people sitting in the Municipal Auditorium in New Orleans waiting for me. Yes, I'd like to speak to the manager.

CAITLIN Dylan, give up. Hang up.

DYLAN (*On the phone*) Never mind.
(*He hangs up the phone. He crosses and sits beside her. They just sit there quietly.* DYLAN *lights two cigarettes and hands her one*)

CAITLIN Shall we call the Municipal Auditorium, Dylan?

DYLAN And say what? "Go home. We're a thousand miles to the west of you"?

CAITLIN Shall we call Brinnin?

DYLAN Poor Brinnin.

84

CAITLIN Poor Brinnin. Well, there's one consolation. Things can't get worse.

DYLAN I don't know. There's still Washington, D.C.

CAITLIN At least, we've got time to get there.

DYLAN That's the spirit. Set your watch.
(The lights go down, then rise on a great Tara-like staircase in the chandeliered foyer of the Washington, D.C., home of the ANTONES, ELENA *and* JAY HENRY. *All are in black tie and tails. Party sounds and music are heard.* ELENA *and* ANGUS *enter from the main door at right.* ELENA *is a well-preserved Southern belle with an accent that sounds like Spanish moss looks)*

ELENA We have damn few great poets nowadays.

ANGUS And precious few great patrons, Elena.

ELENA I hope he likes me.

ANGUS Elena, he hopes you like him.
*(*JAY HENRY ANTONE *enters from the left—a well-meaning Republican elephant)*

JAY HENRY Angus, I think we've acquired an uninvited guest—your assistant is her implausible story.
(Leads in MEG STUART)

ANGUS *(To* MEG) Who's watching the store?

MEG   Who cares! Every spring I have a compulsion to see a cherry blossom.

ANGUS   Sick!

MEG   Aren't you going to introduce me?

ANGUS   Why do I have to always be the one to—oh, all right—Miss Stuart, Mr. and Mrs. Antone.

JAY HENRY   Terrific addition. I'll have Charles bring you some champagne. And, Miss Stuart, hang on, I shall return, as was said by only the greatest man this country ever bred and then kicked in the pants.
   (*He exits*)

MEG   Who could that be, I wonder?

ELENA   (*Who answers rhetorical questions*)   Mr. Antone is probably referring to General Douglas MacArthur. Whenever Mr. Antone's use of the third person masculine gender is in question, it's General Douglas MacArthur, as sure as shootin'.
   (*She exits*)

ANGUS   (*To* MEG)   New dress?

MEG   This old thing? Yes.

ANGUS   You know Mrs. Antone's prepared to give Dylan some money?

MEG   Oh, boss, you don't really trust me.

ANGUS I have spies. I have radar. I have hidden cameras.

MEG Do you also know I've talked to him three times this week and called it off?

ANGUS One time calls it off. Three times shows you don't mean it.

MEG Worry about Caitlin. More to the point.

ANGUS I also thought you were Caitlin's friend.

MEG Wouldn't you be surprised if I turned out to be an influence toward making their marriage work?

ANGUS I would raise both my eyebrows, Meg, for the first time in my life.

ANGUS What does Dylan have to do for the money?

ANGUS Just be friendly. And we are all going to look the other way, *n'est-ce pas?*

MEG So friendly we all have to look the other way?

CAITLIN (*At the top of the stairs*) Meg! You got here. Great!

MEG (*To* ANGUS) I wired Cat if she thought I might come down for Friday's party and Saturday's reading.

ANGUS That was thoughtful.

CAITLIN (*Descending the stairs*) I told her she could come, Angus. She may meet a rich bloody politician in Washington, D.C.

MEG What's Dylan up to up there?

CAITLIN Fussing over his bow tie. Won't be helped. Shot all his time criticizing me as to how I'm turned out. He's a little nervous tonight.

MEG Caitlin, you're beautiful.

ANGUS *Exquisite!*

CAITLIN I don't know why but I've never gotten over thinking a party means something wonderful, unexpected and thrilling is going to happen. Well, Don Juan will be down anon.

ANGUS Now, Cat!

CAITLIN I agreed. I agreed to look the other way. I agreed not to drink. Do I also have to agree to be agreeable?

DYLAN (*At the top of the stairs*) Get out of the way. I'm coming down the banister!

ANGUS Don't tell me he's —?

CAITLIN Since lunch.

DYLAN Wheee! No. I don't slide as well as I used to.

CAITLIN You're overloaded, that's why.

DYLAN Unkind. Unkind. I'm in full possession of myself. I am simply braced to meet the occasion.

CAITLIN Dylan, Meg is here.

DYLAN (*A second stunned, then unable to look her in the eye*) Yes. (*Pause*) Hello, Meg.
(*An awkward pause which doesn't escape* CAITLIN *at all*)

MEG Hello, Dylan.

ANGUS (*Too late to the rescue*) Well. Well. Well, shall we all go join the merry throng? I hear the tinkle of ice and the rending rip of reputations.
(ANGUS *and* MEG *exit.* CAITLIN *remains, watching them go.* DYLAN, *at the door, turns*)

DYLAN Well, how do you want to go in there, Cat? On my arm or over my shoulder?

CAITLIN (*Icily*) Meg.

DYLAN What are you babbling, "Meg"? What's that mean, "Meg"?

CAITLIN What a bloody fool I am, Dylan. How unworthy of your rathood is my naïveté!

DYLAN I don't know what you're talking about.

CAITLIN I think I'll have one drink. It won't kill me!

DYLAN Now, listen to me, Cat, if you lose us our one chance to get the money to take us to Majorca—and patch our poor marriage back together again—I'll never forgive you. That'll be it. We'll be through. Because I've made two killing profitless trips to America and I can't do it again. I mean, this, tonight, is the straw that can break the camel's back. I'm doing this for us!

ANGUS (*Re-enters—interrupting them*) I've introduced you to three people in there already and where are you?

JAY HENRY (*Whipping by and up the stairway*) Gangway, please. I'm going to get my motion-picture camera and catch some footage of Dylan. Oh, hello, Dylan—I'll be right down. (*Sees* CAITLIN) Hello, Mrs. Thomas. My, My!
> (DYLAN *and* ANGUS *go into the party.* JAY HENRY *goes upstairs.* MEG *steps back on*)

MEG Cat, I want to explain.

CAITLIN (*A pause and then, snapping*) How is he? Not bad, is he?
> (CAITLIN *passes her and exits.* MEG *sips her drink, alone for a second.* DYLAN *walks back into foyer arm in arm with* MRS. ANTONE. *She refers now to a marble statue of a naked woman*)

ELENA Well, you walked right past it, honey. This is the one. It was unearthed only last year. It's by Phidias or Praxiteles or one of those early Greek chiselers. Do you know Miss Stuart? Oh, of course you must.

JAY HENRY (*From the top of the stairs*) Baby? Where's my camera?

ELENA Under his nose. I can't come up and find it for you, Jay Henry. I'm talking to Dylan.

DYLAN Are you from the Southern states, Mrs. Antone?

ELENA Memphis. Greek. Wellesley. Republican. Elena. Let's sit on the staircase and get acquainted. Isn't this a wonderful Tara-esque staircase? Yes. It was torn out of an estate in Northern Ireland and imported to Georgia prior to the Civil War. Then, we had it torn out of Georgia in 1928 and brought up here to the capital. They say soldiers have died on it and women have given birth on it and grooms have carried their brides to their nuptial nights up it. And since we've had it, Herbert Hoover's climbed it twice. So let's have a great poet sit on it.

DYLAN Delighted.

ELENA (*Staring at* MEG, *who won't go*) I don't want to have to plunge into that stuffy old party yet, do you?

MEG Excuse me.
    (*She exits*)

ELENA She's too polite, that girl. Her silence is shrieking. She's got something deep on her mind.

DYLAN Angus tells me —
    (BRINNIN *steps on*)

BRINNIN Dylan, you look like a peacock in a penguin suit. There's a Supreme Court justice wants to meet you. He's playing the piano.

ELENA (*Rises*) We must all meet with justice. We can talk later. Come, Dylan. Stand up tall now. Tag, you're it. Take my hand and be led to the slaughter.

(*She and* DYLAN *exit as* JAY HENRY *comes down the stairs*)

JAY HENRY (*Camera and equipment in hand*) Wait up, Brinnin. Would you like to hold the hot lights while I try to get all this down in an imperishable record of film?

BRINNIN Mr. Antone, may I have a word with you? I just had a spur-of-the-moment idea I'd like to discuss with you.

JAY HENRY Sure. Shoot. What's your problem?

BRINNIN Dylan's flat broke.

JAY HENRY I thought he'd been cleaning up.

BRINNIN Well, he had a lot of past debts.

JAY HENRY They can't hang onto it, these artistic people. Somebody ought to go into the arts and make an industry out of it.

BRINNIN He needs a small but sizable amount—about five thousand dollars would do.

JAY HENRY Well, I'd certainly like to be of service. But cash, I mean hard cash, is very hard to come by these days. I'm also completely aware how cruel that remark may sound.

BRINNIN Dylan'd pay it back. He's got a book of short stories he's planning, for which the advances will come to—

JAY HENRY   I tell you. It's always been my observation that you loan a man money, you lose a friend. I'd rather give him the money and forget it.

BRINNIN   Well, the situation *is* pretty desperate.

JAY HENRY   Brinnin, when you need money, it's always desperate. But let's face it. If he doesn't get it from me, he'll get it somewhere.

BRINNIN   Actually, there is a married woman who's offered it but it's a little degrading and I'd hate to have to see him—

JAY HENRY   Listen, if she's discreet her husband'll never know. And if she's halfway cute, Dylan may even enjoy the transaction. By God, I wish I could get my day's work done without getting out of bed. Listen, everything's relative. Only two days ago I was so desperate to lay my hands on twenty million dollars you'll never know! Where was I going to get twenty million dollars? P.S. I got it. From the Mafia, in case you're interested. If you quote me, I'll deny it. There is no Mafia. There you are. What are you gonna do? But still Dylan's a very worthy person, a famous man, a great poet—let me think about it. Five grand's such a small sum—it'd be easier if he needed a million. Right?

   (*He exits.* ANGUS *comes on*)

ANGUS   Are you dunning Daddy Warbucks for the money?

BRINNIN   Why not?

DYLAN

ANGUS   But Elena's practically in the palm of our hand.

BRINNIN   Not if I can help it.
  (JAY HENRY *enters with* CAITLIN *from the main room. She's been drinking*)

JAY HENRY   How many children do you have again?

CAITLIN   Three.

JAY HENRY   That's a lot of shoes.

CAITLIN   Oh, hello, Angus. Isn't it a posh party? (ANGUS *gives a groan of frustration and exits*) Isn't it a far cry from our boathouse in Wales, Brinnin?

JAY HENRY   You want to see *my* boathouse? Brinnin, you want to come look at the Potomac by moonlight?

BRINNIN   I've seen it.

CAITLIN   Oh, Brinnin, you're such a sourball! It's a party!

JAY HENRY   That's the spirit! By God, Mrs. Thomas, you're an extraordinarily beautiful woman.

CAITLIN   Well, I'm glad somebody noticed.
  (*They exit out the front door.* DYLAN *comes on, glass in hand, smoking*)

DYLAN   John, come join the party, dear boy. I must be five drinks up on you.

BRINNIN   Dylan, I've spoken to Mr. Antone about getting the money for you and he's considering it.

94

DYLAN That's a laugh. Too bad you can't tell him it's self-protection. That's if I can ever get alone with her to bring the subject up. Have you seen Cat?

BRINNIN She just went out to look at the Potomac with Mr. Antone. (DYLAN *gives him a look*) Oh, now, Dylan!

DYLAN She's higher'n a kite. If that old goat lays his foul fiscal fingers on her, I'll bust his pompous head open.

BRINNIN Easy. Easy, Dylan. I'll go join them. Don't be rash. Hang onto your purpose and stay on your feet.

DYLAN It's a war of nerves. The bloody woman fights me at every turn.

BRINNIN You don't make it a bed of roses for her, Dylan.

DYLAN I'll show her. Get out of my way. I'll end it once and for all.

BRINNIN Dylan! You've got an empty glass, Dylan. Sit down on the steps with your empty glass and let five minutes go by without pouring alcohol into your bloodstream.

DYLAN I need to be clear-headed, don't I?

BRINNIN Please. And I'll catch up with Cat. She loves you, Dylan.
(BRINNIN *exits. A* GIRL *runs on*)

GIRL Is Dylan Thomas at this party?

DYLAN No.

GIRL   I crashed the wrong party. Thanks. You don't know where he is, do you?

DYLAN   He's home in Wales.

GIRL   Isn't he gonna read tomorrow night in Washington?

DYLAN   No. They're using a recording. His wife is going to stand up and mouth the words.

GIRL   Will that work?

DYLAN   You'll never notice the difference.

GIRL   Excuse me. Peter, what do you think I just heard! (*She exits.* ELENA *comes down the stairs*)

ELENA   There you are, Percy Bysshe Shelley.

DYLAN   At last—alone. On the steps of the Library of Congress, I imagine.

ELENA   You need a little pot of gold, I hear. How much?

DYLAN   Five thousand. I can pay it back by—well, within a year. Absolutely.

ELENA   Oh, you pay it back any time you can. I'll give you a check.

DYLAN   When? I keep losing you.

ELENA   Now. Where?

DYLAN   How do you mean where?

ELENA I mean we ought to slip away to some private corner. Someone might misconstrue.

DYLAN Where would be good?

ELENA My bedroom. That'd be good. We can lock the door.

DYLAN Two adult people can lock a door without there being any more to it than that.

ELENA I admire the pants off you.

DYLAN I like you, Elena, too. I'm terribly taken with you.

ELENA Would you have liked me if I hadn't a penny in the world?

DYLAN Without question!

ELENA I'm so glad you said that. Come.
(JAY HENRY *comes on*)

JAY HENRY Elena, leave me alone here a bit with Dylan. I want to talk to him.

ELENA Oh, Jay Henry! Just when he was flirting with me outrageously. Dylan, raincheck?

DYLAN —Uh—check!
(*She goes*)

JAY HENRY Look, uh—Dylan—uh—Brinnin let drop the fact you're a little embarrassed. Financial straits and so forth. He's not out of line, is he?

97

DYLAN   No. I do need some cash fairly quickly.

JAY HENRY   Yes. Well. I can't make head or tail of your poems but I do like mightily the way you read 'em. What's your politics over there?

DYLAN   Politics?

JAY HENRY   You know. Tories versus the Whigs or whatever's going on over there these days.

DYLAN   My politics? I see what you mean. Anti-Stalinist.

JAY HENRY (*Narrowly*)   How you mean?

DYLAN   I mean I'm in favor of the worker as opposed to the exploiting bosses. I'm in favor of feeding the hungry, curing the ill, destroying all armaments everywhere and tearing down borders between people. I'd also like to do away with money. And do you know any nice Negro girl I can marry off my son to?

JAY HENRY   No wonder you're broke! Why, man, that's the talk of a Communist sympathizer. How the hell did you ever get a passport into this country?

DYLAN   All the Democrats in Congress got together and snuck me in.

JAY HENRY   I believe it! Goddam! Where's Brinnin? Where's that Marius guy?
(*He storms off.* BRINNIN *and* CAITLIN *come on from the front door*)

CAITLIN   I am *not* drinking too much. Brinnin, you're a spoil sport.

DYLAN   Brinnin, Jay Henry's hunting high and low for you.

BRINNIN   Did you talk?

DYLAN   We had a very pleasant chat—about politics!

BRINNIN   My God!
(*He rushes off.* DYLAN *and* CAITLIN *are alone*)

CAITLIN   I have a marvelous idea. Why don't you get the filthy money from Meg? Then you won't have to split your focus. Why are you staring at me?

DYLAN   What the hell ever became of that girl I met in Augustus John's studio that day?

CAITLIN   I think I'm going to dance.

DYLAN   You can't dance.

CAITLIN   I can dance. You used to love to watch me dance. I have reminded certain people of Isadora Duncan from time to time.

DYLAN   Of Isadora Duncan too goddam drunk to dance.
(CAITLIN *begins to dance—it's like an awkward four-year-old child. She simply lifts her dress up over her head and turns in dizzy, slow circles. Several people move in from the party to watch.* ELENA *comes down the stairs to* DYLAN, *who rises.* ELENA *takes his hand and draws* DYLAN *up the stairs.* MEG *enters.* CAITLIN *looks at* MEG *and stops dancing. Suddenly* CAITLIN *spins, sees* DYLAN *with* ELENA *and tears up the stairs*)

CAITLIN (*Spelling the word*)   Where the s-h-i-t do you think you're going with him?

DYLAN (*Roars*)   Caitlin!

CAITLIN   I'll tear her hair out. The dirty bum has to pay to get laid!
(*She flails at* ELENA)

ELENA   What's the matter with her? Is she mad? What is she saying?

DYLAN   The money was for Majorca. You forgot the purpose of it! I'll kick you down these stairs, Cat!

CAITLIN   Try it! I can beat you up, Dylan, and you know it. You whore! Come on! What *are* you? Come on! You son of a bitch! Come on!
(*He lunges at her, and* CAITLIN *pulls him down with her—in the process kicking two struts out of the imported banister.* ELENA *screams.* CAITLIN *and* DYLAN *are now roaring insults, rolling on the floor wrestling, kicking, slugging each other. Everybody stares aghast.* BRINNIN *and* ANGUS *tear on last and stop to gape. The lights go down. A spot on* DYLAN *alone that widens gradually to reveal him in a doctor's office*)

DYLAN   I'm me. I smoke too much. I drink too much. I never like to go to bed. But when I go to bed, I never like to have to get up! I sleep with women. I'm not much on men. Necrophilism—that's with dead bodies—leaves me cold. I never watch the clock and it doesn't pay much attention to me. I write poems and I read 'em out loud. I lie, I cry, I laugh, I cheat, I steal when I can. I must have an iron constitution as I've been abusing it for years to an extent which'd kill a good horse in a matter of hours. I love people, rich and poor people, dumb as well as smart people, people who like poetry and people who never heard of poetry. I'm life's most devoted, most passionate, most shameless lover. I must be. And I like a good party and a good time and applause and lots of pats on my back and pots and hats full of jack which I then like to spend without stinting. Comforts make me comfortable; nails in my shoe, an ache in my tooth and grit in my eye do not. I have lived in a time when men have turned Jews into soap. I've been, I must tell you, ever since those days, a wee bit confused about the godly nature of the human creature. But I'm not as confused as anyone I ever met or heard of. Because I am me. And I know me. I've sung a few songs in thirty-nine years just for the pleasure of singing, but now I have come to a point in my life when I think I have something to say. I think it's something about having the guts to thumb your nose at the social shears that clip the wings of the human heart in our mushrooming, complex, cancerous age. I'm hot for fireworks in the dull of night. I want the factual, killing world should go back to fancy kissing for its livelihood. I'm about to write an opera with Stravinsky. A play on my own, my first, called *Under Milk Wood*. And I've been offered to play the lead in a play on Broadway. Things are looking up. But I'm spitting a lot of blood and blacking out more often than I'm used to, and I think I had a touch of the d.t.'s this past week as I've started seeing little things that aren't there—mice, for example. Miss

Meg Stuart, my friend, suggested that I come to see you, Doctor, as it's entirely possible and not a little ironic, now that things are finally looking up—(*Long pause*)— that I'm dying.

DOCTOR   Mr. Thomas, you're lucky you're not dead.

DYLAN   My God.

DOCTOR   Wet-brain. That's the popular term for it. An insult to the brain from too much alcohol for too long a time. The little blood vessels in and around the gray matter are shorting—like an electric circuit. Those are your blackouts. If too many more of them pop, you've had it.

DYLAN   You mean I'm—exploding, by degrees, like a star?

DOCTOR   Do you really want to live, Mr. Thomas?

DYLAN   Yes.

DOCTOR   One would never know it. You have a wife and three children?

DYLAN   In Wales. My wife's gone back to Wales.

DOCTOR   Why don't you go home to them?

DYLAN   No.

DOCTOR   Mr. Thomas, if you take one more drink—a small drink, a beer, a sip—you will have committed suicide as surely as if you'd jumped off a cliff or shot yourself in the head or swallowed a suitcase full of barbiturates. Now, those are the ground rules. How you want to play the game is up to you. Your life is in your hands.

According to what I read in *Time* magazine, you're reported to be the greatest lyric poet of the twentieth century. Doesn't that obligate you?

DYLAN   I'm not so good at obligations.

DOCTOR   Are you a great poet, Mr. Thomas?

DYLAN   I don't know. I'm just me. I'm me.
(*The lights go down; then come up on the basement of the Y.M.H.A.* MEG *and* BRINNIN *come downstairs.* DYLAN *at a table is writing furiously*)

MEG   He's down here in the basement. I think he's almost done.

BRINNIN   Dylan!

DYLAN   (*To himself*)   Polly Garter cries longingly, "And I'll never have such loving again."

BRINNIN   Dylan. The auditorium is full up, up there.

DYLAN   I'm reading this over. Hello, Brinnin. Be right there. Right there.

BRINNIN   Good God, you swore you'd be all through writing it the afternoon I left for Boston. What have you been doing for two days?

DYLAN   Brewing it, stewing it, putting in commas. Meg, darling, another Coke for the good boy.

BRINNIN   You're really on the wagon, I see.

DYLAN   Yes. Yes. World of good for me. I'm a completely new chap. My arm is a pincushion from the doctor's shots and I've pills to take that were made for elephants and I'm sick to death of Coca-Cola but I'm alive, after a fashion.

BRINNIN (*To* MEG) How much has he got to go?

MEG Dylan, how near done are you?

DYLAN Few pages.

BRINNIN Look, for the purpose of the reading right now, why don't I just state it's incomplete and you can find a good stopping spot in what's already done.

DYLAN No, got to finish.

BRINNIN The natives are restless.

DYLAN Let them wait! Five minutes.

MEG. The cast though, Dylan, is pretty nervous upstairs. They know they're going to get new pages handed to them at the last second.

DYLAN They're professional actors—they'll have the pages in front of them on the rostrums. It's just a reading, not a Broadway production, and it's all one-syllable words, besides.

BRINNIN Was there ever a play so thrown together at the last second?

DYLAN I'm reading six parts personally. Stop worrying. What's that?
    (*All three glance up at a thunder from the ceiling*)

BRINNIN   A thousand people stamping their feet. It's almost nine o'clock.

(NANCY, a young actress in the cast, appears at the head of the stairs)

NANCY   Dylan, come on!

DYLAN   Patience, Nancy. John, go up and assure everybody I'm judge-sober, all-present, full of sixteen hours of sleep from last night. I've only to write curtain and I'll be up 'n' spouting at 'em.

BRINNIN   Well, I'm not going to let them know the thing's being written ten seconds before they hear it.

DYLAN   Why not? Create a feeling of spontaneity.

BRINNIN   I'll give a long introduction. In two minutes, Meg, done or not.

MEG   He'll be there.

DYLAN   Tell them how I've met my master in my mistress and have turned a new leaf.

(BRINNIN exits up the stairs)

MEG   How can I help?

DYLAN   Do you see a matchbook around here? With two lines on it?

MEG   This one?

DYLAN   No. It's the beginning of the Reverend Eli Jenkin's sunset prayer. Just before the town's about to go to bed at the very end of the play.

MEG (*Picks another*)   Hotel Algonquin?

DYLAN   I think it was Minetta's I was in, having a glass of milk.

MEG (*Reads*)
"Every morning when I wake,
Dear Lord, a little prayer I make"?

DYLAN   That's it. (*Writes as he speaks*) "Every morning when I wake, dear Lord, a little prayer I make." The pencil broke! Goddam it to hell!

MEG   Here. Here. Here's one nice and sharp. Where's the rest of the prayer?

DYLAN   In my head—somewhere. I can't do it. It takes too long to write it out.

MEG   I'll get it in shorthand. Go.

DYLAN
". . . prayer I make . . .
O, please to keep thy lovely eye
On all poor creatures born to die."

MEG   Good enough.

DYLAN   There's more.

MEG   You'll do it on the platform.

DYLAN
"Whether we last the night or no
I'm sure is always touch and go."

MEG   "I'm sure is always touch and go."

DYLAN
"We are not wholly bad or good
Who live our lives under Milk Wood." Got it?

MEG Got it.

DYLAN Wait. I lost my opening pages. They're the only copy. I left 'em in a cab yesterday and the blessed cabby found me out and returned them. Here they are. Who spilled coffee on that? Is my bow tie straight?

MEG In terrible taste and crooked. Come on.

DYLAN What am I going to do at the party after when everybody's drinking?

MEG You're going to be the famous man, Dylan, in the corner with the glass of soda water in his hand.

DYLAN Oh, God, Meg, thank you! Thank you! I think I've got a hell of a chance.
(*The lights go down. In the dark, a cresting surf of applause, the approval of the thousand attendant at the Y.M.H.A.'s first reading of* Under Milk Wood *and spiking through the tide of sound like intermittent splash of praise: "Brilliant, thrilling, a world, the language, the language, the language!" The sound of the ocean is heard. The lights rise at stage left on the beach in Wales and the boathouse.* ANGUS *is at the foot of the stairs*)

ANGUS Caitlin! Haloo!

CAITLIN (*Appears at the top of the stairs and calls down*)
Is that you, Angus?

ANGUS I'm in London on business and trained out to see you. I've got to be back in New York for Christmas.

CAITLIN Don't come up. The house is a wreck. I'll get a coat and take you to Brown's for a decent drink.

ANGUS Hurry up!

> (*She goes in.* ANGUS *lights a cigar. At stage right the lights rise on a Christmas tree trimmed and lit in a corner of* MEG'S *apartment.* MEG *and* BRINNIN *are there tossing the last of artificial snow on it*)

MEG Get a little more on those branches there. He'll be angry that we didn't wait for him, but that's just too bad.

BRINNIN Did he say where?

MEG If you mean is he at the Horse, he may be but he's sipping Coke if he is. That's law.

BRINNIN I feel as if I haven't seen him in a month of Sundays. I hope he understands. If he's going to live here the year around, I've got to earn a living.

MEG It's *been* a month of Sundays—quiet, pasting the good reviews of *Under Milk Wood* in his scrapbook, eight hours' beauty, lots of milk, Dickens and Bartók and the only living alarm clock in captivity—me.

BRINNIN Terrific for him, Meg.

MEG Oh, we forgot to put the star up. Do the honors, while the man of the house is absent, would you?

> (BRINNIN *takes the star and* MEG *steadies the kitchen steps for him. As he climbs up,* CAITLIN, *in*

a coat, descends the stairs to the beach in Wales, to
ANGUS, *who kisses her hand continentally)*

ANGUS   Bless you, Caitlin. So this is Dylan's corner of Wales. At last.

CAITLIN   That's the shack up there above the house where he scribbles himself half-blind. How is the bloody man? Is he coming home for Christmas?

ANGUS   Well, he's—you know—the good reading of *Under Milk Wood* was a big springboard for him. Now there's an offer for this, plans for that. The future's bright.

CAITLIN   He's not coming home for Christmas.

ANGUS   Ah, but surprise. I come bearing good tidings. From Dylan. Open it. Open it.

CAITLIN   (*Taking an envelope from* ANGUS)   What's in it? One of Brinnin's blue envelopes? (*She rips it open*) It better be money.

ANGUS   A check for a thousand dollars. Count the zeros. (CAITLIN *sits on the steps*) What's the matter? A shock to the nervous system?

CAITLIN   Don't talk to me for a minute. Please.
        (*The lights rise at center stage as the* BARTENDER *leads* DYLAN *to a table and chair in the White Horse Tavern, as* BRINNIN *has set the star up, descended to the floor to* MEG *and slapped his hands together)*

BRINNIN   I am not as incompetent as Angus Marius thinks. You see that.

MEG   Angus is going to see Cat in Wales. I removed a thousand dollars from Dylan and sent it along with him.

BRINNIN   I bet that'll be welcome the expensive time of the year.

MEG   Let's have eggnogs. Shall we? No, you sit and grow a beard. Take me a second.
> (*She exits.* BRINNIN *picks up a book and leafs it*)

BARTENDER   Boy, we haven't seen *you*, Dylan, in a dog's age.

DYLAN   I'd like eighteen whiskies, please.

BARTENDER   Off the wagon?

DYLAN   And a Coke. I just want to look at eighteen whiskies. That's the world's record, you know.

BARTENDER   Boy, you're an original. I'll bring 'em on.
> (*He exits.* DYLAN *takes his coat off. At stage left* CAITLIN *is crying—just sitting there tall, and the tears falling down her face*)

ANGUS   Can I loan you a very new handkerchief? I thought you'd be delighted as apple pie!

CAITLIN   Is he still at the Chelsea or has he moved in with company?
> (BRINNIN *on his side of the stage*)

BRINNIN   Meg, is Dylan still at the Chelsea?

MEG (*Off stage*)   Absolutely.
> (ANGUS, *on his side of the stage*)

ANGUS   He's still on the register, Cat.

BARTENDER   Here you go, Mr. Thomas. Take a long look, but don't jump in, the water's awful.
   (*He sets the tray of drinks down in front of* DYLAN)

DYLAN   Right.

CAITLIN   So, this is the way we're going to finish it—in a warring absence.

MEG   I don't know where he can be.
   (*Hands eggnog to* BRINNIN)

BRINNIN   Here's to Dylan. Wherever he is, there are no tears.

MEG   I'll buy that.
   (*They drink*)

ANGUS   Come now, Cat. No more tears. Blow your nose. It's just a temporary alliance that's probably going to do a world of good.

CAITLIN   But a bloody check is such a hollow wonder.

BRINNIN   Great eggnog. Why don't we call the Horse?

MEG   I have to trust him, John.

JOHN   Then, let me call.
   (*He goes to phone and dials*)

DYLAN   (*To himself—softly, in memory*)   "I want to be the drunkest man in the world."
   (DYLAN *begins to build a pyramid of jiggers like a child with building blocks*)

CAITLIN I have the curious sense I'll never see him in this world again.

ANGUS Nonsense!

BRINNIN (*On the phone*) This is John Malcolm Brinnin. Guess who I'm looking for. He is? Please. (*To* MEG) He's there.
(BARTENDER *crosses to* DYLAN)

ANGUS I tell you, you'd be really extremely proud of him, Cat. He's stopped drinking. He's a man coming into his own, in every sense.
(BARTENDER *whispers in* DYLAN'S *ear*)

CAITLIN Without me! Without me!

DYLAN (*Shakes his head to* BARTENDER) No! I'm not here. You made a mistake. It's not really here that I am, anyway.
(BARTENDER *goes*)

MEG (*To* BRINNIN) See if he seems sober. I don't want to get on with him. But if he's had a drink we'll catch a cab down there immediately. Don't tell him that.

BRINNIN (*Nods and then on phone*) Yes?

ANGUS (*To* CAITLIN) Let's go to Brown's and have a Christmas cheer. We'll drink to Dylan. What do you say?

DYLAN (*Softly, alone*) "You look at the pyramids; I'll look at the Bible."

Alec Guinness as DYLAN

BRINNIN (*On the phone*) Thank you. (*He hangs up. To* MEG) I don't believe him. Now he says it was some-body looked like him.

MEG Oh, my God! Let's get out of here! I just have to get my coat.
(MEG *runs off stage*)

CAITLIN (*To* ANGUS) All right. Oh, let me put on the Christmas-tree lights. (*She goes back upstairs and snaps on the lights of a little ratty fir tree atop a table at the head of the stairs*) I know really he'll come back here somehow. Wales is his home. He loves Christmases. (*She comes down the stairs*) He's like a little boy about them. Maybe he'll, at the very last minute— (*And she reaches* ANGUS' *side*) —find a way to come back.

ANGUS (*Offering his arm*) That's how to look at it. Dylan knows what's best for him.
(MEG, *back on with coat, joins* BRINNIN)

BRINNIN Maybe I never should have invited him to America.
(*As they exit, ocean sound is heard.* CAITLIN *looks out to sea, across the Atlantic*)

CAITLIN (*Calls*) Dylan! Dylan!
(*She smiles and exits with* ANGUS. *The lights go out both at stage right and at stage left. The large Christmas tree in America goes slowly dark. Only the little Welsh tree stays lit, high up with its shining star on top. The pool of light on* DYLAN *enlarges*)

DYLAN (*To himself*) Christmas! Thirty-nine, twenty-nine, nineteen, ten, Christmas! "Hit him with a snowball! Look at your footprints. People'll think there's been hippos here. Merry Christmas!" Jim and Dan and Jack and me! "I wonder if the fishes ever get to see the snow. That's the brightest star over all of Wales! Good night! Good night!"

Father in Heaven, Mother of God, bless, curse me now from that sad height. I love you! But I'm alone! The rage of the world! Half-compromise, half-lie? *I'm coming home!*

(*He spins and snatches the top drink off the pyramid and tosses it down. Another. Another. Another. He leans on the table to support himself. He gasps for breath. The tears are running down his face. The lights go out at center stage and the Christmas tree gets intensely bright just before it fades to dark. Boathorn and ship's bells are heard in the dark. The lights rise. It is a starry night aboard ship. CAITLIN is seen standing on the upper deck. Below the deck is the hold of the ship. In a dim light, trunks and boxes and coils of rope, and a sizable crate are seen. A young ship's OFFICER appears and approaches CAITLIN*)

OFFICER Good evening, Mrs. Thomas. I apologize for the Atlantic in the wintertime.

CAITLIN (*Abruptly*) I'd like to see where the bloody dead man's kept.

OFFICER (*A trifle taken aback*) Yes, ma'am. (*He starts toward the steps*) This way, ma'am. (*He goes ahead of*

her, leading the way down the steps) The cargo manifest says he's in storage-hold number ten.
(*They reach the hold*)

CAITLIN (*In a belated apology for her brusqueness*) I'm no good at grief. (*She goes into the hold and stares at the large crate*) I can't seem to be pleasant about it. Is that it? Is he in that?

OFFICER Yes, ma'am. It's got a little tag on it with a number.

CAITLIN Is naught a number? Or a total lack of number? I can't remember. How lucky he is—to be the first to go. (*Then quietly sardonic*) "Who here knows my husband, Dylan Thomas, the poet?"
(*She starts to go*)

OFFICER (*Matter of factly*) "Do not go gentle into that good night."

CAITLIN (*Stops and looks back at the wooden crate*) Yes. "Old age should burn and rave at close of day. Rage, rage against the dying of the light."

OFFICER (*Simply and unrhetorically*)
"Tho' wise men at their end know dark is right
Because their words had forked no lightning, they—
Do not go gentle into that good night."

CAITLIN (*Gradually having come to stare at the* OFFICER) Do you know the damn thing by heart?

OFFICER Some of it, ma'am.
"Good men, the last wave by, crying how bright
Their frail deeds might have danced in a green bay."

CAITLIN (*To herself*) I'm taking him back to that green bay.

OFFICER "Rage, rage against the dying of the light." (*He glances up at her—is embarrassed*) Excuse me . . . I'd better get back.
(*He exits*)

CAITLIN Thank you . . . yes, thank you. (*She turns back to the box*) Isn't it amazing? All the years, nights with his arms folded, when he lay asleep, I used to say to myself, why the bloody man's not a man at all—why I'm married to a child. But you'll come off better'n any of us, Dylan . . . in a thousand years. And you planned it, too —dirty Dylan!
(*She strikes the box with her fist, then rises and goes up the stairs to the upper deck of the ship, and turns toward the audience, gripping the railing and looking off into the sea and sky and the winking stars, which are also timeless—as* DYLAN's *journey to America ends*)

CURTAIN